BEYOND ART

*What Art is and Might Become
if Freed from Cultural Elitism*

BEYOND ART

What Art is and Might Become
if Freed from Cultural Elitism

ROGER TAYLOR
Lecturer in Philosophy,
University of Sussex

THE HARVESTER PRESS. SUSSEX
BARNES & NOBLE BOOKS. NEW JERSEY

First published in Great Britain in 1981 by
THE HARVESTER PRESS LIMITED
Publisher: John Spiers
16 Ship Street, Brighton, Sussex

and in the USA by
BARNES & NOBLE BOOKS
81 Adams Drive, Totowa, New Jersey 07512

© Roger Taylor, 1981

British Library Cataloguing in Publication Data
Taylor, Roger, b, 1940
   Beyond art.
   I. Title
   700.1
BH221.G74T

ISBN 0-85527-143-4

Barnes & Noble Books
ISBN 0-389-20205-3

Printed in Great Britain by
St Edmundsbury Press, Bury St Edmunds, Suffolk

To Marlene

Contents

I would like to thank Maggie Boden,
Terry Diffey, Barry Selwyn, Richard Wollheim
and my wife Marlene for their advice,
encouragement and assistance
during the production of this book.

1

Introductory remarks

Today many people enjoy a wide range of dancing, film, literature, music and visual art. The range includes established art, *avante-garde* art, primitive art, folk art, and the products of popular culture (e.g. pop music, commercial cinema and T.V. serials). This book attempts to reveal the human dimension that is basic to all these experiences, the dimension of 'as ifness'.

Rather than arguing that catholic interest in the range results from more things being art than is recognised officially (the main theoretical explanations of the phenomenon are of this kind), I maintain that it is what art shares with life beyond art that makes art important. In accounting for the difference between what people enjoy now and what used to be the case one must look, of course, for social explanations, but the main thrust of this book is in the direction of uncovering something basic to the nature of what is enjoyed. What is basic is a necessary condition, in this case, of the social determinants being able to determine as they do. Bringing to light this basic dimension shows what is beyond art not just in the sense of what lies outside, but has affinity with, art, but also in the sense of what form of existence might supersede art.

Art is seen, in my argument, as one of a range of equally important embryos from which a more highly evolved form of existence might emerge. To argue in this way is timely, because recent younger generations have failed theoretically to understand the radical nature of their practice. Many forms of life have gone beyond art, but when seeking understanding of what has taken place there has been a falling back on outmoded theories of art. This book tries to correct this mistake by making the 'as if ' its central concern, and not art.

In an earlier book (*Art an Enemy of the People*[1]) I argued (to put it crudely) that art *qua* art is no more than a specific bourgeois process and that what makes art art is no more than the conferment of the label 'art' by the appropriate social

1

process. This is so despite it being believed, within the process, that it is not so, and that the category of art is built on objective standards. These facts taken together lend a degree of incoherence to the practices of art. This thesis is justified on the basis of the whole practice of art being a recent historical product (mainly from the eighteenth century onwards) rather than a universal practice. Jean Gimpel's *The Cult of Art*[2] and Raymond Williams's *Marxism and Literature*[3] argue for a similar position. To discuss art in this way is very much to see it from the outside; but what of the point of view of the devotee?

For the devotee, Bach (for instance) is understood in terms of personal confrontation with his music, not against the background of involved social processes. The significance of asking whether something is a work of art or not, or of asking the more general question 'What is art?', pales beside the thought that regardless of whether it is art or of what art is, the experience of Bach's music is a vital and enriching part of a person's life. Now, one objective behind this book is to lend credence to this suggestion without restoring status to the category of art. This is something which needs doing because the various art *forms* (forms which very importantly encompass more than the instances of art) do indicate a coherent human practice, despite the way they are involved in the incoherent processes of art. In my view, activities like storytelling, play acting, painting, dance (activities which when distilled in a particular way yield the range of art forms) do have a common base, which when considered as a general phenomenon can be shown as something basic to being human. It is in terms of entering into *this* human dimension that particular experiences, such as the experience of Bach's music, can be understood. However, to say this is to do nothing to reinstate art as a coherent human practice, and the reason for this is that art is a malformed sub-class of this more general human dimension. Thus, I shall argue that the enriching experiences within art grow out of what it shares with what is beyond art. A consequence of this is that there are many things (particularly within the various current manifestations of popular culture) that can in no sense be located within art but which have the same importance as art objects. Moreover, art objects do not have this importance because they *are* art.

This book then, grows out of wishing to give some account of experiences internal to art; experiences which are not peculiar to art but are peculiar to the general category of which art forms a sub-group. Of course, much of the internal experience of art is determined by the social and historical setting in which it occurs; it is not as though internal and external dimensions of art are independent of each other (in fact a detailed study of how they are part and parcel of the same thing would be illuminating[4]). Despite this, there is some residue from the internal experience which cannot be fully analysed in terms of interconnections between internal and external perspectives, and it is only by subsuming this residue under the general category ('as ifness') that it can be understood.

Something of an introductory nature needs to be said about this general category or common base. Is there anything sufficiently general we may say about the relationship between the art object and its admirer? Certainly there is involvement, and an entering into. There is a transportation by means of, a sense of transcendence, a sense of being convinced by. The experience is compelling. One's attention is captured. One forgets oneself, even though the work may seem to integrate one into it, and the sense of this having happened is something integral to the whole experience. What is dropped, or forgotten, are the concerns or preoccupations with which one comes to the experience; or, if the experience organises them, what is dropped is the way they weigh with one. Skimming something off the detailed accounts to follow, we may say: in reading fiction we feel something is being made real for us; the poem brings something to life for us, it evokes its subject; the theatrical experience gives us a sense of having been transported into another reality (a reality other than the theatre in which we sit); the painting is something which absorbs and transforms us through its representational qualities; a piece of music seems to organise the environment in accordance with its own structure, and its own structure is something we interpret in what I will call for now 'representational' (if rather indefinite) awareness. These transformations are brought about by the convincingness of the objects responded to.

The extent to which the words I have chosen would be chosen by others to describe their experience of art objects in general terms is open to query; but I belive some such description is fundamental to giving an account of this experience. A prolonged justification of this belief will appear in subsequent chapters. What we do not have in this very general description is an account of the particular character of the transformative and convincing thing Bach's music is. But then, one should not expect it. If the general description seems too weak it will be because one's expectations are for something that does more justice to the specific experience. If some such general description is in place then it is clear it is not confined to the way we respond to art objects. It may be that the description tells us more about the *experience* of art than an account of the conditions under which the art list is made (the social and historical account of my earlier book), but it is just as informative about the experience of some non-art objects (e.g. popular culture objects). Thus, it is a central feature of the film that neither is nor tries to be a work of art that it be transformative through its convincingness. The general phenomenon to which I am trying to direct attention I call 'as ifness' and the main category of objects displaying 'as ifness', which includes art objects, I shall call 'entertainment objects' or, more in line with common usage, 'entertainments'. These terms plus derivatives will be used frequently throughout this book. I shall maintain that 'entertainment objects', in contrast to art objects, constitute the relevant class of important and interesting objects. My demonstration of the importance and interest of this class will involve giving a full account of the ways in which we create and respond to the 'as if'. 'As ifness', therefore, is the coherent object sought in the demands made of the art forms.

As an early indication of the meaning and plausibility of the idea that 'as ifness' is something central in what is sought of art, some concentration on a maximally simple situation is instructive. I wish to draw attention to a minimal residue left over when the temporary social significances have been extracted. This is not to say that such a process of refining can be actual; what is really intended is an analytical speculation. One way of approaching this is to try to think through the minimal basis on which a new art form would be possible. This approach provides a glimpse of how 'as if' considerations, rather than other considerations, confer prima facie plausibility on the suggestion that some new activity could constitute an art form.

It is a fact about painting and music that our experience of them demands the use of particular senses. On what basis might an art form be invented for the tactile sense? The fact that some sculpture has a tactile component, in the sense that it requires the use of the sense of touch upon it, does not make the invention unnecessary. The tactile sense employed in the sculptural setting is exploratory in nature, whereas the tactile sense functions as often in a passive role. The invention, then, might be restricted to directing something at the tactile sense. Music begins with the musical instrument even if the instrument is the human voice. By analogy, some instrument with which to affect the tactile sense might seem a promising starting point. Suppose someone were to build a 'tactilator', what kind of a thing could it be? In the diagram below is a possible suggestion.

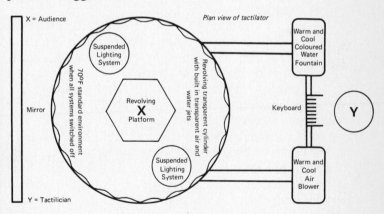

From the diagram it will be apparent that the 'tactilator' is a machine that is capable of producing jets of water and gusts of air, both at varying temperatures. For a given volume, it can direct these jets and gusts at that volume as it is directed to do by the 'tactilician' (the performer). The jets and gusts can be *played* (here the analogy with musical notes is being worked hard) for as long or short a duration as the tactilician wants. What is to be played is ultimately determined by 'tactiles' (equivalent to the piece for performance in music), which may be composed beforehand and written down in some suitable notation. The audience is limited to one person who, for maximum exposure to 'tactiles', waits nude for the piece to begin. The cylinder, nozzles and tubes are all transparent so that the performer can direct the tactile sensations to those parts of the body specified in the score. To facilitate his seeing the side that is not directed towards him a mirror is positioned at the other side of the cylinder. It must be borne in mind that to compose a 'tactile' is, at least, to think about promoting certain tactile sensations in the audience. In other words, it would not be enough to give instructions concerning the position of the nozzles and the frequency of the jets and gusts.

In addition to this description of the 'tactilator' and its functions, we can note some of the factors that the composer of 'tactiles' would need to take into account. It should be apparent to the composer that it is possible to instil rhythm into the tactile sensations produced (the analogy with music continues). Further, it will be possible to give sensations a special identity by producing them in one place and then moving them without interruption to another place. In these circumstances the audience will build up beliefs about similar sensations occurring in different places at the same time, and about the same sensation remaining in the same place throughout a duration, or of its moving throughout a duration from one place to another. No doubt the composer will have to take into account the facts about the different reactions which are set up, which depend upon the parts of the body stimulated rather than on the nature of the stimulus. These are some of the factors which composers of 'tactiles' would have to consider. With more time and more ingenuity more would be forthcoming.

However, apart from the way in which the analogy with music holds, it is unclear whether as yet we have a description of an art form. Perhaps we have a description of a contraption that might have a profitable use on the fairground, or in Soho, but not much more. To imagine oneself within the instrument, being blown at and squirted upon, seems far removed from the experience of art. But then, if all we had was a musical instrument and no notion of what music was like it would be just as difficult to see how instances of an art form could be performed on it. If this were all we knew, we could see no more in the musical instrument than a machine for making noises with. What is required, therefore, in judging whether or not the potentialities of the 'tactilator' encompass the possibility of a new art form, is some clear understanding of a 'tactile'. We could try thinking about the transposition of a musical piece into 'tactile' form as a guide to a 'tactile' of which it would be sensible to ask if it was a work of art. The rhythm of the musical piece could be transposed exactly. Supposing a piece for the piano was chosen, the treble could be confined to the air and the bass to the water. The ascending and descending order of the notes could be mirrored by directing the jets and gusts to the upper and lower parts of the body. However, the situation is still unclear, though we might surmise that our tactile sense is not a good enough receptor for the kind of finessing which goes on in music.

What though if the experience of the 'tactile' can be described as follows? It is as though one is in free fall, like just having jumped from a plane. One revolves slowly on the platform, and the air streams up over one's body from one's toes, uplifting one's hair. It is as though one enters a gusty pocket of air, there is buffeting, and then one comes through to glide, though still revolving, through soft streams of cool air. Then the first suggestion of the earth. There is a hint of rain through scrappy spray, there is a circular feeling to the air as though a breeze may be getting up off the sea and bringing with it spray. And then there is water up to one's midriff; one sinks and the water is warm. But there is a sense of movement. One has ceased revolving and warm air comes from behind horizontally. The movement of the water conveys a sense of one's moving in a certain direction. But then the current runs cold, the air is cool, the water is cool. There is a suggestion of polar regions, and then there is a gradual fading of all sensations. The 'tactile' is over.

This description gives a crude indication of the 'as if' potential of the 'tactile' as well as making plausible the suggestion that this is an idea for a new art form. The nature of the experience promoted by the 'tactile' is significantly like experiences which other art forms provide, although the likeness is expressed differently, in so far as the 'as ifness' seems necessarily egocentric, whereas, for example, in the theatre the dramas enacted concern others and not oneself (or at least, this is the normal pattern). Of course, it will be important to ensure that the nature of the tactile experience does not overstep certain limits. For instance, the cool water and air, in the polar passage of the 'tactile', should not be so cold as to be distressing. If this were to happen one would be too concerned with how one actually was for it to be *as if* one were drifting through polar regions. It will also be important that the tactile sensations produced should compel an 'as if' understanding of them, and it will therefore be insufficient to recognise that the experiences resemble other experiences one might have; it will need to be the case that one finds it unavoidable to think about the experiences *as if* they were other experiences. This last point is a reference to 'magnetic as if' situations, the general nature of which is dealt with in chapter 3.

Until arriving at an account of the transformative and convincing character of the 'tactile' (what I am calling its 'as ifness') there was only an account of a bizarre machine, plus some purely formal analogies with the structure of music. With the 'as if' characterisation there is, in terms of the intuitive feel of the case, a much closer approximation to the standard art forms, and therefore the semblance of a reason for thinking that something central to art has been indicated. This theme will be explored in depth in chapters 4 to 9, where various attempts will be made to show how an 'as if' characterisation is basic to the particular art forms of drama, literature (in general), visual art, music and dance. However, before this is possible it is necessary to give some account of the 'as if' in general, so that what at present must seem obscure ideas become intelligible: this is one of the projects of chapters 2 and 3.

My main objective in this book might be stated quite simply, namely, to give an account of the 'as if'. To do this one section of the book is given over to a specification of the grounds on which the 'as if' arises in consciousness, as well as giving an account in the process of the general features of the 'as if'; the next section deals with an analysis of a number of common 'as if' objects, and the last section is concerned to understand how we respond to the 'as if' and the role it does, and ultimately may, play in our lives. The interest of this as a project is, of course, impossible to assess until the notion of the 'as if' has been properly introduced. As I shall explain in chapter 3 the notion of the 'as if' in Vaihinger's writing is quite different, and any anticipation connected with that context would therefore be misplaced.

Despite this being the main theme, for the purposes of understanding this book it has to be set against another theme. Something coherent is sought of art (the 'as if'), and it is something which needs preserving from the myths of art so that arguments for the qualitative superiority of art do not emerge. It is the way in which these various topics coalesce which accounts for much of the detail of this book. This is to say that the coalescing of topics gives rise to many areas of contact between the particular ideas I wish to advance and the various standard topics in philosophy, aesthetics and critical theory. By my itemising these various points of contact at the outset it will be possible for the reader to anticipate areas of familiar discussion and interest, which will be thrown up within the context of more unusual ideas.

In general, the points of contact are twofold. Firstly, there is the range of theories concerned with our ideas and projects and their connections with the world we inhabit and experience. A particular manifestation of this is the way in which, according to a very persuasive and influential theory, our products are to be evaluated depending upon whether or not they correspond to the world. The point of contact here is with the various arguments I offer to separate the 'as if' from reflection and previous experience. Secondly, there are a number of theories (some just philosophical and others theories of visual art, literature and music) which by implication either challenge the characterisation of the 'as if' to be offered here or challenge the notion that our art forms have a basic connection with the 'as if', a connection which explains what is central and coherent in the internal experience of art. All of this is, naturally, by implication, as the concept of the 'as if' is peculiar to this book.

In more detail the connections are as follows:

(1)   Empiricism, idealism and Romanticism all have consequences for the theories of imagination, creativity and what I
am calling the 'as if'. Empiricism inevitably ties the created
entity to the range of previous experiences, and thereby
construes the work as being reality-directed, if only in an
attenuated sense. In opposition to this I argue that our
creativity presupposes the ability to think that which is new,
where this is not just the composite of old experiences. This
argument is advanced by means of exploring various defi-
ciences within empiricism. A consequence of the argument is
that the 'as if' object is released, at a very basic level, from
being interesting as something reality-oriented. In opposing
empiricism, the barest logical plausibility is given to the idea
that the 'as if' is a parallel development to life, in a sense
similar to Bradley's famous contention about poetry. This
theme is followed up substantially in other sections of the
book. The worry about the connection between the created
product and reality obviously involves some consideration of
Romanticism, in so far as part of the discussion is concerned
with the sphere of art. For instance, there is the problem of
the intentionality of the product and any implicit biographical
reference that may be involved. These problems take the
form of how intentional the 'as if' object has to be and to what
extent it must be interpreted as an expression of its author.
My own argument is for some understanding of the notion of
'creative act' which is independent of the notion of intention,
and for creative interpretation treating the 'as if' object as
public and thereby open to public manipulation (thus not
logically tied to biographical explication). The Romantic
theory of art is not primarily a philosophical theory about the
concept of art but more a theory of value, which by implication would argue that the 'as if' would only be valuable if in
accord with this theory of value, and that what was in accord
with the theory would fall within the sphere of art. For this
reason Romanticism offers a defence of art which is opposed
in some of the later sections of the book. Idealism comes into
consideration obliquely when I characterise my own theory
about the creative process as a variant on some aspects of the

ontological implications of the idealist theory of art. Despite this the main bulk of idealist theory is rejected.

(2) In trying to characterise the art forms as exhibiting 'as ifness' and in characterising 'as ifness' in terms of what seems to be but is not (this is a synoptic presentation of the views to be argued for) one looks for plausible challenges (again necessarily by implication) to these ideas. One oblique challenge is provided by J.L. Austin's account of pretending, an account I extend to the theatre. This account does *not* demand that *what seems to be the case be not the case*. I try to refute various argumentative possibilities in this account, just as, in considering drama in general, I challenge the incoherent thinking behind various contemporary attacks on traditional dramatic forms. Another oblique challenge, although this time the philosophical literature on the subject does centre itself within philosophical aesthetics, is the view that fictions either contain no propositions with truth values or contain propositions all of which are false. The nature of this challenge is less intuitively than logically apparent. If 'as ifness' is related to some notion of convincingness (an idea to be introduced later) then the alleged fact that works of fiction contain no true statements has to be accommodated in some way, for it might seem, from a purely logical point of view, that an account which has to be convincing cannot be full of false statements or contain no statements at all. I advance a view of fictions as containing propositions most of which have to be judged true. Moving from obscure to more direct opposition there are several areas of contact which are covered. Firstly, there is the standard thesis of philosophical aesthetics that notions of *form* explain the interest which is taken in art. This formalist thesis is opposed in its strongest areas, namely those of visual art, dance and music. The argument is that what pass, in the theory, for formal properties are on analysis 'as if' features. Secondly, there is the challenge to 'as ifness' in visual art which comes primarily from Gombrich's denial that a representation works through its looking like what it is a representation of. The view is explored in depth and its defects, as I see them, analysed. Thirdly, and lastly, a challenge to the view that poetic imagery assists the 'as if' status of poetry is dealt with by means of an

attempt to resolve the old dispute between Hulme and Richards on the subject of the nature of poetic imagery.

(3)   The third general area of contact overlaps with the first, being concerned with the relationship between the 'as if' object and reality. I argue that though there is no valid qualitative distinction between high and low culture this is not to say there is no way of distinguishing between successful and unsuccessful 'entertainment objects'. The criterion employed is one of convincingness (properly understood). As soon as this idea appears so, by means of coupling art and truth, it is possible for the ideology of art to make a reappearance, for it might seem that convincingness must be measured in terms of truth and that works of art have some monopoly of this factor. It is the attack of this particular defence of art which is undertaken most seriously in this book and, I suspect, permeates most of its pages. The theme is explored in giving consideration to the writings of Abrams, Brooks, Danto, Hospers and Kermode, amongst others. My general line of argument is that convincingness is not to be understood through correspondence, and that works of art themselves are not assessed as successful through considerations of correspondence, and that even if they were there are serious doubts as to the validity of such assessments in so far as there are doubts about whether works of art can correspond to the world at all.

(1) to (3) give some indication of points of contact between the ideas of this book and a range of standard subjects. There are other possible points of contact which, for various reasons, are not taken up explicitly in this book. Firstly, there are real parallels between my ideas and those of Marcuse in *Eros and Civilisation*[5]. Marcuse's celebration of play and his strictures on the repressive nature of reality-dominated thinking are both close to various conclusions I argue for on grounds other than those based in psychoanalysis. Secondly, there is a close connection between my rejection of the defence of art, where this defence is based on the grounds of its alleged cognitive concerns, and Raymond Williams's ideas in *Marxism and Literature*, especially so in his chapter entitled Literature. Finally, the defence of art as some kind of cognitive activity gains a special kind of support from Marxist

aesthetics, and the defence in this form receives only an outline treatment in this book. For a sustained attempt on my part to bring out the deficiencies of Marxist aesthetics I refer the reader to my chapter on this subject in *Art an Enemy of the People*.

Although this work has the ostensible subject of the 'as if', and thus has an idiosyncratic subject matter, it does grow out of a dissatisfaction with art and aesthetics, and is therefore deeply rooted in considerations of these areas. So although this is not intended as a standard work in philosophical aesthetics, it uses the interests of this area (mainly by challenging them) as a springboard to thinking which goes beyond art. This I would like to relate to a particular social phenomenon which has grown up in recent years.

It is typical today to find amongst younger people with intellectual dispositions a stiff resistance to cultural élitism. Typically, in my experience, if younger people are asked what kind of painting, music or literature they like they are inclined to indicate that their taste is catholic, ranging across the accredited instances of art as well as the instances of popular culture. When pressed to account for possible inconsistency implied by their preferences there tends to be a defence along the lines that *it is all art*. This seems to me a very typical social attitude, particularly present amongst university students. The widespread nature of this attitude makes it likely that culturally a conceptual shift has taken place, whereby the concepts of art and culture have been extended to cover areas not previously admissable. The usual pattern of extensions has been one of radical gestures by the producers (the artists), whereas what we get primarily in this instance is a radical shift by the consumers. A number of factors account for this, including the established commercial domination of what is called popular culture, the multi-class complexion of higher education compared with how things used to be, and the fact that, given the acceleration of, and thus the exhausting of, radical gestures by the producers within the established tradition, raiding popular culture was more radical than any other possibility. To ransack popular culture was, however, to be determined by its commercially and technologically advanced production forms. Therefore, the radical shift in consumption carried with it a packaging of the objects consumed and an interest in the objects as packages. Despite these socially determining factors it is not possible to reconstruct from them the full internal experience of the various objects responded to. Of the factors listed, the factor which comes closest to explaining and describing the internal experience is that of the radical feeling that went with listening to the Grateful Dead or the Eagles or whomever, where the feeling was that this listening was on a par with listening to Beethoven or Indian music, etc. If one reflects on this for a moment, I think one can understand how the radicalism was reinforced by liberal feelings. However, to have described this much is not to have explained the transportation of oneself which the experience involves. By 'the transportation of oneself' I mean something as simple as the state one gets into when listening to the Rolling Stones, for example. The social group I am dealing with tends to explain this internal experience by invoking the concept of art, although the concept is by this invocation expanded.

The 'explanation', however, only has the form of an explanation. For when one seeks some elucidation as to how the idea of art explains the experience, usually no answer is forthcoming, as though the use of *art* as a value imposes some ultimate explanation. Of course, aesthetics attempts an elucidation, though in my view unsuccessfully, but those who invoke the concept of art are largely unaware of this. It is in this way that art as a value functions ideologically, in the sense that a conceptual structure is utilised as an automatic social reflex in place of a real understanding of one's interests, consciously thought through. As a result of this, both the felt need to challenge élitism and also the discovery of areas of interest beyond traditional cultural boundaries are dissipated in the lame rationalisation that it is all art. In fact, despite the democratic intentions involved, the discriminating aspect of the concept or art is retained, because the concept is withheld from *very* commercial, *very* low cultural objects. Although the intention in employing the concept in the first instance is not to exclude them, they are not even in mind.

The ideas of this book can be related to this social phenomenon as an attempt to articulate the nature of the internal experience so as to avoid falling back on the clichés of art. The social impulse I have been describing is, as I interpret it, an attempt to break through an oppressive form of life to something beyond it, but it tries to do this without theoretical effort and therefore when it tries to come to know itself it relies on standard conceptual reflexes. My own enterprise takes its motivation from this same social impulse, but I have tried to recognise the need for theoretical transformation. Grandiloquently then, this book aims at producing, in one area, the sort of theory that a whole generation requires — and requires because when in need of theory it has turned lazily and uncritically to outmoded theoretical equipment. A preoccupation with the 'as if' is what really typifies the interests I have been describing. This is not to say that such an interest is confined to a particular generation; it is just that the expansive range of objects that this interest has sought out in recent generations exposes it from its concealment within the art process. For these reasons, therefore, this book is about the 'as if', about how the 'as if' is possible in consciousness, about its nature, status and possibilities and about how it connects with art.

In conclusion I would like to work back to some of the ideas I have been dealing with by means of a brief consideration of Williams's *Marxism and Literature*. Williams's book contains an epistemological muddle, and although this is not the deficiency I am aiming at it does lead on to themes with which I am concerned. The muddle is both simple and common. The notion of being able to say how the world is, or to state the facts, Williams sees as a socially produced delusion (positivism, empiricism, etc.). The thought that we can understand the world as it is does not (according to Williams) stand up to the scrutiny of changing cultural process and the changing filter of language. The thesis can, of course, be given substantial documentation along the lines of work by people like Kuhn[6] and Feyerabend[7], but the muddle appears as Williams strives for a methodology, where methodology is what he requires to understand social process (though it is stressed not in any abstract, static way). This is a contradiction, though not one of manageable dialectical proportions. The contradiction is that we must be careful not to falsify yet we cannot get it right anyway. This contradiction is not readily apparent in Williams's text because, as no positive view of things is offered, it manifests itself only as a methodological recommendation. What appears positive in Williams text are correctives to erroneous conceptions. The position *appears to be* one of not being in the world. The position is one of standing outside and scrutinising the falsifications, false abstractions as well as indicating the social tensions which make the falsifications understandable. This position of standing outside gives Williams's book a lack of concreteness. It is clear what the book is saying in general terms, but it is unclear why there is a concentration on culture, literature and art. The category of art and literature as the highest category of human expression is not only dismissed by Williams but is identified as a local, historical product. These views do not really justify the long-standing interest Williams has displayed in the category, except in so far as they contribute to a proper understanding of an area of social life. Moreover, the interest goes further than just establishing the general thesis, it extends (at least in theory) to locating each particular development of the category and even to each particular instance within the category. But is this sort of analysis necessary? There might be an answer at the level of Williams's interest being in communication or the use of language; art, culture and literature being part of the history of this. Certainly, Williams's range encompasses semiotics, linguistics and media. We might say that art, literature, etc., are just one form communication has taken (although we have, following Williams, to be careful with 'form'; this is very much the methodology, i.e. whenever we glimpse understanding we have to be careful we have not over-formalised lived existence, life as 'constitutive practice'). Thus, the differentiation between art, literature, etc., on the one hand and the range of various academic forms of communication on the other (e.g. philosophy, science), though real, in the sense that such differentiation has occurred, is seen as an unnecessary fragmentation (in an abstract, theoretical sense) of the possibilities of communication.

However, experience of art from the outside like this makes experience of it from the inside very difficult. If somehow the individual can encompass both attitudes the problem is one of relating them to each other. Is being engrossed in a novel compatible with the external, knowing attitude? Or, is it the case that the external, knowing attitude exposes one's gullibility? For instance, Williams analyses things like place and character in the novel through considerations of conventions and social attitudes, i.e. we see works utilising conventions where the conventions are indicative of more general social facts. For Williams, interest in a novel is very much conveyed at this level and so the notion of getting lost in a novel disappears from view. Perhaps what is going on here is that the ideology of art, and the kind of interest which goes with it, predetermine the sort of interest retained in art after the ideology is exposed. This is to say it is part of the ideology of art to maintain that art is cognitive; if this is undermined (if only on the basis of epistemological relativism) and yet one clings to cognitive enterprises (not now fulfilled by art) then penetrating art as evidence of social truths takes over from art just speaking the truth to one. But, now, something has dropped out, i.e. *being involved* with an instance of art, though this experience may not drop from view, as it can itself be dealt with as a piece of social data. Much Marxist treatment of art works like this and although Williams distinguishes himself from standard Marxist analyses he does this only on the basis of depicting the crudeness of the other analyses (e.g. crude interpretations *vis-à-vis* base/superstructure models). In other words he distinguishes himself by the sophistication of his trace back for cognitive significances. Williams does not investigate how it is possible that the novel can be experienced as engrossing. This sort of primitive fact, which can be a fact about any novel, is very much the subject matter of my book, although my subject matter is more general than primitive facts about the novel.

Similarly to Williams, standard literary criticism in concentrating on the text, style, aspects of content, etc., does not provide any general account of the reading of fiction as a distinct kind of reading. There are, I shall argue, primitive facts about the art experience (although they are not confined to the art experience) that explain something of the possibility of the engrossment that goes with reading novels, or looking at pictures, or listening to music. Moreover, these facts, when understood, allow for engrossing experiences that are independent of possessing the sort of social attitudes which can be connected with the detectable conventions of the work.

2

Imagining and the empiricist-creation theory

Imagining involves imaginary awareness, or, to make the point more pretentiously, involves making it as though something is impinging upon one's consciousness when it is not. Thus, if a man is imagining x then this involves him in making it as though x is impinging upon his consciousness when it is not; this is having imaginary awareness of x. If this is the case, it explains why one cannot both be aware of something, and be imagining that same something at one and the same time. For example, I cannot both be having a pain in a particular area of my finger, and at the same time be imagining myself having a pain of the same intensity, rhythm and spatial position. One way of showing the necessity of the connection between making it as though something is impinging upon one's consciousness when it is not, and imagining that something is, is brought out by a short excursion into the views of the philosopher Berkeley.

Berkeley thought that perception was a necessary condition of a thing's existence. He regarded unperceived entities as a contradiction in terms. This is something which in the *Principles of Human Knowledge*[8] he undertakes to prove. One method he adopts is to ask whether it can be conceived that a thing exists (i.e. whether we can spend our time imagining a thing existing) without it being conceived that it is being perceived (i.e. without imagining it is being perceived). Berkeley's claim is, then, that we cannot spend our time imagining the one without imagining the other. If Berkeley is right in holding this then he presents not an insignificant reason for thinking that the perception of, and the existence of, a thing are logically inseparable. One method, which is not irrelevant in trying to show that a certain state of affairs is logically impossible, is to make an appeal to what is imaginable, or an appeal to what you can make appear to be the case even though it is not. If the state of affairs is logically impossible, then it will not be imaginable, conceivable, possible, to make it appear to be the case.[9]

It is clear on one interpretation that Berkeley's claim is false, i.e. if his claim is that x cannot be being imagined without it being true that x being perceived is also being imagined. But on another interpretation, I think, his point can be maintained. This interpretation would be that one's imagining x entails it being as though x is impinging upon one's consciousness. If we insist on this latter interpretation we find it fails to yield the consequence Berkeley was after. The difference between these two interpretations is brought out if we distinguish between *one's imagining* and *what one imagines*. It is impossible that one's imagining does not entail it being as though something is impinging upon one's consciousness, though it is clearly possible that what one is imagining is something not being perceived, i.e. something not impinging upon anyone's consciousness. I think Berkeley failed to make this distinction. He realised imagining involved imaginary awareness, but did not realise that the imaginary awareness involved did not constitute an aspect of what one was imagining. Thus, that which is true and necessarily true of the activity of imagining is not thereby true of what one is imagining. Perhaps an example is clarifying. Suppose I am imagining a bird flying over a green field. To do this is to do something distinguishable from imagining a boy observing a bird flying over a green field. Certainly, I can spend my time imagining one of these things or the other; it is not as if, in imagining a bird flying over a green field, I have to imagine also an observer of the bird's flying. However, in imagining either of these scenes I shall be having imaginary awareness of them; it will be true that it will be as though these scenes are impinging upon my consciousness. However, I shall not be imagining that it is as though these things are impinging upon my consciousness, rather it will be that my having imaginary awareness will constitute my imagining, it will not be what I imagine, it will be the imagining of it. This necessary truth is insufficient to establish that the perception of a thing is a necessary condition of its existence. If two things are logically inseparable then something which indicates that they are will be our not being able to imagine the one without the other. We can, however, imagine something, or other, without imagining someone perceiving it. Thus, I can imagine a bird flying over a deserted field, or to be in no way controversial, I can imagine a large stone in the middle of an otherwise deserted field.

Of the two phrases I have been using (1) *it being as though something is impinging upon consciousness when it is not*, and (2) *making it as though something is impinging upon consciousness when it is not*, the latter is to be preferred though it contains ambiguities. The thought of *making it as though* contains the intentional ingredient necessary in an analysis of imagining, and therefore excludes the experience of natural illusions. That it does not exclude illusions one might inflict on oneself can be taken care of by insisting on a special sense of *making it as though*. Thus, there is the sense which covers manipulations of the environment, and the sense satisfied by the mere presence of a volition plus the possession of appropriate psychological equipment. Clearly it is the latter sense which is required. This characterisation of imagining helps to clarify the relationships between imagining itself, *imaging* or visualising and projection.

Not all imagining involves *imaging*. For instance to sit in a room, whose contents have not been altered or rearranged for ten years, is to provide oneself with ample opportunity to make it as though it is then and not now, or to make it as though now is then, without the aid of *imaging* or even projection (in any visual sense). The quasi-transition, in terms of oneself, might involve banishing contemporary thoughts where they would be in conflict with the past, and reviving the thoughts of the past at the same time as colouring them with their one-time urgency (e.g. 'How am I going to propose this to her?'). There are other comparable cases. Thus, I dance in my room as though I were the great Nijinsky, I imagine I dance as well as he did. I do not project, I do not *image*, I merely ignore the faltering of my untrained toes and my toppling sensations. In this instance exclusion is as potent a device as invented additions.

Turning to imagery and projection, what kind of distinction is required between the two, and do both necessarily involve imagining? To have a visual image is to seem to see both item and its context, but this is not to say either need be pure figments of the imagination. On the other hand projection requires that either the item or its context be actual. The phenomenological difference between these experiences is that in the first case we are likely to locate the experience as just within the mind, whereas in the second case the metaphor seems inappropriate. But now what of the connection with imagining?

For some thinkers *imaging* is a frequent, though frequently interrupted, occurrence. *Imaging* is reported to be an integral part of their thinking. This is not to say their thinking is accompanied by vivid flashes or by that kind of spectacular private show associated with drugs, rather thinking of a man, for some people, proves difficult without seeming to see him in the mind's eye. However, in describing thinking which contains these moments then it is incorrect to refer to imagining as the activity engaged in. Something more is required if we are to describe correctly a person as spending his time imagining something. The more is a matter of attention and volition. If I am asked to think of a person I may seem to see his face, and this may well be so despite myself, despite say, resolving not to. If, on the other hand, I am asked to hold this experience of seeming to see then I begin imagining. This happens as the face I seem to see begins to stare back or smile or twitch or something. As I prolong the experience its content becomes more complex; the means to this complexity involves attention and volition. So it is this special volitional sense of *making it as though something is impinging upon consciousness* which separates mere *imaging* from imagining. Thus, suppose someone describes to one a state of affairs in which sides of beef grow on their hooks while dripping blood. The descriptions might be so evocative that one seems to see at times the state of affairs described; however, none of this is imagining until one allows oneself to wander between the sides of meat to reach out and touch them. At this point one makes it as though these things impinge upon consciousness. In this connection projection can be seen as a way of imagining, and therefore as being unlike *imaging*, except in so far as projection is a feature of some hallucinatory experiences, in which case to speak of imagining is misplaced.

Given this characterisation of the activity *imagining* it is possible to proceed from this basis to see how we can give some account of the way it intrudes into the production of instances of art forms and the 'as if' in general. Before doing this, however, there are certain theories about connections between imagination and art which must be sketched in. These other theories will be sketched in only to exclude them. At least one of these theories needs critical attention; it will not receive it now, although it will be returned to.

There are two theories which advance crucial relationships between imagination and art. One I will call the *ontological theory* (though it is but *an* ontological theory), the other the *empiricist-creation theory*.

The ontological theory holds that a work of art's mode of existence is in a mode of consciousness. It exists in imagination. The work of art is an object of imagination. This theory is very much the theory of the Romantics[10] and very much the theory Collingwood[11] gives us, though he was borrowing heavily from Continental sources, e.g. Croce[12]. The limitations of this theory are ably set out by Margaret Mcdonald in her article 'Art and Imagination'[13], where the main line of attack centres around showing that a distinction can be maintained between real and imaginary instances of art forms that the ontological theory obscures. Despite acknowledging these limitations, it is possible to see the account I shall give as being a variant on this ontological theory.

There are the folloing points of difference at least between the ontological theory and the empiricist-creation theory. Firstly, the empiricist-creation theory is founded on what purports to be a theory of imagination, namely the compositionalist or empiricist theory of imagination.[14] The ontological theory does not need a comparable support. Secondly, the empiricist-creation theory aims to explain how a work of art or any human product for that matter is composed or produced, whereas the ontological theory seeks to explain in what form the work of art exists. It is the empiricist-creation theory which needs critical attention and to which I will return.

There is another account of a connection between imagination and art which needs to be removed. It hardly merits the heading 'theory'.

This view is mundane. The view is that the production of art objects involves us in producing something new, something which goes beyond our previous experience of art objects. Where this is so whoever produced the object can be said to have used his imagination. To say of a man (in this sort of context) that he used his imagination is to say no more than this man came up with something new. The role played by the assertion 'he used his imagination' in the English language, does not have to reduce to the analysis, 'he produced this new or unique thing by using some faculty, which he has, called imagination'. The role played by this assertion in the language is quite compatible with the analysis 'he produced some new or unique thing'. The view here is that common usage approves the connection long before we begin to concern ourselves with theories about the connection. There is reason to see the empiricist-creation theory as providing a theory to explain the given connection. That the connection is given, is trivial; that the given connection is explained by a certain theory, is not trivial. It is to this that I shall return.

Having put these theories to one side I shall maintain that for certain things, here are certainly included music, fiction, drama, painting, sculpture, architecture, ballet and opera, the activity of imagining is characteristic of their production. As a prior move to showing just how imagination is involved I shall make some remarks about thought and consciousness.

What will you be thinking about in five minutes time? Sometimes this sort of question is difficult to answer, at other times much easier. In cases in which we can predict what we will be thinking about, can we also predict that what we predict will be all we shall be thinking about at the given time? There are activities like reciting which can be performed parrot-fashion. Here one can predict what will be the object of one's consciousness in fifteen minutes from now. But, where the activity is performed with such ease, how can we prevent other thoughts from occurring? This difficulty is related to that of not knowing how to be conscious while having nothing in thought. Consider next activities which are taxing, which absorb us. To characterise activities thus, is to say they take us beyond our anticipations. Instances of such activities are writing fiction, composing music, painting, working out the multiplication table for whatever number you find taxing, solving chess problems, doing an I.Q. test.

There is a difference between not knowing what I am going on to, and not knowing how to go on. Mental activities which can be performed automatically can involve us in problems of not knowing what we are going on to. Mental activities, which involve difficulty, involve us in not knowing how to go on at times. If I do not know how to go on, I will not know what I am going on to. At any moment in the creation of an art object or 'entertainment object' there may arise situations in which one will not know what one is going to move on to. Such situations may be complicated or inflamed by our not knowing how to go on. But now, how does one move on? What is involved? What is involved in completing the tune, in concluding a certain passage in the first movement of the symphony, in moving from a spiral of red and green lines to the left of the figure to blue and yellow ones to the right, in moving from the incident where she sits under the tree to the incident where an old Jew comes to join her? Part of the answer, at the philosophical level, is that one is able to move on by *creative acts*. The creative act is yet another topic I shall take up later. But as this answer emerges so does another question, namely, 'how does one perform the creative act?' Does one's hand simply go to the chord and strike it, and then does one recognise what one has done and judge it, or does one first have to think the progression of the chord sequence? Does the tune first have to be in my head before it can be sounded on the keyboard? Or, if I sound the tune on the keyboard, and the tune is one I compose, does this guarantee that the tune is in my head? Whether or not the tune is in my head prior to my striking its notes may be an unimportant question. What does it matter if it is in my head as I strike the notes? The tune being in my head is not the same as my hearing the tune. A tune may come to be in my head as the result of hearing the tune. Certainly it would be suspicious if the tune came into my head only as the result of my striking its notes. Would I then be its composer, or would I have learnt a tune as a result of extemporising, or as the result of an accident? Extemporising is not composing. I can extemporise without attending to the music I make: there is a certain way of playing a musical instrument which is very like assembling components on the factory bench: it is a matter of making physical movements within existing musical rules. But we would not call this composing.

As I create music, the music is in my head. But what does it mean to say this? The difference between a man who fills his staves with notes but is surprised (totally) by the performance of these notes, and a man who fills his staves with notes but is not surprised (he thought it would sound like that), is the difference between a man who has not imagined hearing the music and one who has. Is not the music being in one's head a matter of imagining hearing the music? Is not the music being in one's head a matter of it being as though it is impinging upon one's consciousness, a matter in the case of composing of making it as though it is impinging upon one's consciousness?

It would be rash to forego the question marks above. Let me direct attention to a passage from Wittgenstein's *Blue Book*. He says,

We could perfectly well, for our purposes, replace every process of imagining by a process of looking at an object or by painting, drawing or modelling: and every process of speaking to oneself by speaking aloud or by writing.[15]

There is nothing here about musical composition, but it is not difficult to see how these comments become relevant. This passage from Wittgenstein yields a point of view, but not the argument behind this point of view. It would be to exceed the bounds of relevance to do the argument justice. Instead, I shall give only a sketch of the views involved.

The main contention is that the process of imagining as a necessary precursor of a performance (e.g. making the promise, extending the hand) is an irrelevance. The idea that we would not know how to proceed unless we had first imagined ourselves proceeding as we eventually do proceed, is discounted by pointing out that the very same difficulties which perplex us when we think of how it is we can move from one stage of a performance to another, affect the performance of the process of imagining. The process of imagining does not explain how it is we can move on, rather it presupposes what some might think it explains.We are next invited to make a test for ourselves. For instance do we get the feeling in conversation that first we say the words to ourselves and only then utter them? Clearly enough the answer is 'no', we do not do this.

In extending the argument to musical composition it is easy to see the form it will take. The process of imagining hearing the sounds can be deemed unnecessary, it is enough that we reach out and play the notes. All of this is, I think, satisfactory as long as we concentrate on the question, how is it that we are able to proceed, how is it that we are able to move from this stage of the performance to the next? Against this question the process of imagining seems an irrelevant factor. But I have hinted as much. When I came to the question of how it is that we know how to go on, I claimed the answer at a philosophical level rested with the notion of the *creative act*: a notion to be dealt with later. But it was claimed as we come by this answer we come by another question, namely, 'how is the creative act performed?' An account which will not do is that we just discover that we have performed it. This is to say it will not do to dispense with the question. It will not do to say it is done unwittingly, such that we do not detect any characteristic thinking involved. It is a distortion to say we discover we have performed the creative act. We do not learn of our performances; it is more accurate to say we think them. One does not come to know one's tune by striking the keyboard and listening to sounds that are made, though playing it over and over may help one to exclude something or complete a sequence. The tune one composes is not some physical measure of one's performances as is the racing driver's lap-time. There is another question here, i.e. a question over and above knowing or not knowing how to go on. The question is, 'how does one come to know what it is one is doing?', or similarly, 'what makes the performance one's own?' The answer appears as we take hold of the suggestion made a moment ago. We know what we are doing by thinking it, the performance becomes our own because it results from thinking. Clearly enough speaking is not like switching on the tape-recorder, and composing is not like sitting down at the pianola. But in what does this thinking consist? It will not do to say it consists of uttering intelligible sentences, or playing coherent musical sequences.

The answer wanted must relate the performer to his performance. The inadequate answer just given simply restates the performance. On the other hand, the explanatory thinking will not be a casual mechanism, at least it will not be an antecedant necessarily. The reasons that might make us offer it as such have already been discounted. I am not offering 'thinking' in the spirit of dualism. I am offering it because I can see no other way in which the correct kind of self-awareness can be guaranteed. Despite this, it would be wrong to conceive of the thinking in the case of speaking, as taking the form of a silent saying, but then linguistic thinking, where there is no public saying, does not have to coincide with imagining hearing a voice, whether one's own only muted, or that of another. To insist here that a silent saying is the only thing which will do, is like arguing that the only thing which will do in the case of composing is the composer's hearing a full-scale orchestra. How we are to characterise thinking in words falls outside my present interests: I doubt in this case that the characterisation must involve the process of imagining something or other. However, when turning to the more relevant question, namely, how we are to characterise musical thought, then it seems nothing other than imagining hearing the music will do. Certainly thinking of the notes in a mathmatical way will not do. Music is sound, and sound cannot be translated as words can. Imagining hearing the music will be compatible with not imagining its source, e.g. trumpet, human voice or what have you. The naturalness of what I am saying comes out if one thinks of whistling under one's breath. Suppose the tune is a familiar one. The impression one gets is of a perfect rendering of something tuneful. However, it is clear if we listen to the noise we actually make it is without tune, the nearest it will get to what one is rendering will be in rhythm. The gap here must be filled by the thinking involved, yet it is clear that the feeling we get about what thinking is involved, in a performance such as this, is that it is not distinct from what goes on when we go to the piano and compose.

Consider next painting.

Consider painting with an absence of judgments of the following kind, punctuating the process of creation: 'I think perhaps a patch of blue there', 'the yellow will intensify the tone without becoming a pictorial constituent', 'the chin needs more modelling, it needs to be more rounded'. I might simply paint, looking but not judging; my actions are either completely random, or if selected, selected not in accordance with pictorial demands. Alternatively, I might paint allowing judgments of the following kind to mediate: 'This yellow is revolting: remove it', 'I must erase these fuzzy lines', but, on the other hand, all positive acts with the brush are as in the case where I make no painterly judgments. These two cases are not importantly distinguishable from cases where monkeys, or machines, have been set to work with brushes. It does not much matter whether or not the products of such activities are found pleasing. I shall assert only that they lack a creator. One must be positive about painting. One has to decide what one will add to the composition. Wiping out a mistake in a painting is not just a matter of removing a line, it involves finding a new line, thinking about which line will work.

In music one can extemporise. In painting something similar is possible. Watch the cartoonist at work. He does not hesitate. He relies on memory and habit. The schemata for his figures is pre-established. He can draw you a face, which is often good enough for his purposes, without really looking at it. Where one's painting is directed by a creative process one must be in a situation where one asks 'how will it look?', 'what will it look like?' Thinking of how blue will look there, will be imagining how blue will look there, making it as though blue there, is impinging upon one's consciousness. One solution to 'how will blue look there?' is to put it there; it must be the best way of finding out what one wants to know. However, for the painter getting the question and putting it seriously before himself is already to have been imagining blue there.

The mental process involved in painting is not like: think of a place phrase for a place on a rectangular figure. *Right hand corner*. Think of a colour word. *Red*. Think of a shape word for a patch of colour. *Round*. Try a round patch of red in the right hand corner. Even if this process correlated with what are deemed aesthetically satisfying products it would not be the mental process of the painter.

In some contexts moving from not knowing what is wanted to knowing requires logical thought, calculation, working out and not imagining. In some contexts the latter activity would be an irrelevance. For example, in a practical engineering test I may look at the arch, calulate stress and decide that a rigid steel joint should be inserted. I do not have to spend my time imagining the arch with its support. In painting the problem is one of how it will look, or what will look right there. To think about what will look right there is to be imagining how things will look there. In fact one may say the form in which one gets one's idea of a thing which will eventually be there exhibiting such and such a look, is one of making oneself seem to see it there. All of this is compatible with the state of affairs in which one's anticipations are upset; when it is there exhibiting that look.

Consider next fiction.

I shall distinguish between the writing of fiction and making up fictions. The first involves seriously taking on the project of writing a short story or novel. The second is a device for extricating oneself from a hole, a matter of finding an excuse. Not imprecisely one can spell out the difference by saying, in the writing of fiction one appears, but only appears, to make empirical claims about the world which cannot be true of it, whereas in making up fictions one does make (or one comes to make) empirical claims about the world which are meant at most as only appearing true of the world. Now the difference between the logic of these situations points to the intrusion of imagination as an activity in the former case, but not necessarily so in the latter. The writer of fiction cannot simply be concerned with stringing together a number of fictions. He must make it appear that he is making empirical claims about the world when he is not, and when we know he is not, i.e. he has to give us a convincing impression that he is. If you are unwell you may have only to say ''I'm not well you know' to make me think of you as a sick man, but if I know you are well and that you are out to give me a convincing impression of being ill, you will have to do a lot better than 'I'm not well you know'. The more in the case of writing fiction is to make real what you write about. To know you are doing this, that you are succeeding, is to make it real for yourself as you write. It is your success at this that as a writer you judge yourself. Making it real for oneself as one writes is making it as though what one writes of is impinging upon one's consciousness, i.e. making it real for oneself is imagining it.

In very general form the claim I am making about the creative process can be put like this: there are questions about the origination of what one gets out of creative thought, but there are also questions about how what is got out is thought. In the latter case the phrase 'mode of thought' is helpful. For some things the individual comes up with, the mode of thought involved is not to be regarded as a dispensable vehicle. Moreover, if you analyse out our performances so that imagining is not necessary to anything we do, you are left with something which we can do, but which is totally redundant, i.e. a special capacity completely lacking a function. This is strange. Moreover, there does seem to be great prima facie plausibility in saying that our ability to think of what is not present is at the base of our being able to think creatively.

I shall now return to examine what has been introduced as the *empiricist-creation theory*. I think this theory has some grip on most persons who come to think about creativity. Certainly, this is the most famous theory about connections between unique products of human thought and imagination. The aim in what follows is to weaken eventually the grip which this theory may have on our minds.

Human thought begins, to state the empiricist thesis in a somewhat anachronistic though very intelligible terminology, at the point of experience of internal and external impressions (sensations and percepts).[16] The having of impressions gives rise to ideas. The complexity of just how this happens can be omitted. Ideas we hold in us. Simple ideas constitute our memory of impressions. Complex ideas on the other hand may constitute our memory of impressions, or may constitute the products of our minds which have reflected either on simple ideas, or on complex ideas which are memories of impressions, or on complex ideas which are not, or on a combination of all three. Complex ideas which are not just memories of impressions are produced by imagination. In some versions imagination is both the storehouse of what ideas one already has, and the power to work on the ideas one has to produce complex ideas which are not memories of impressions; in other versions imagination is the latter only.

This point of view sees imagination as an ability or power that human beings possess to produce complex ideas that are not memories of impressions. The ability is exercised in reflecting on, combining, composing from the ideas one already has. The empiricist view is that the complex idea produced via an exercise of imagination will be analysable into an atomic structure of ideas, all of which constitute memories of impressions. In other words the complex idea must be capable of being broken down into that which one knows directly or by acquaintance.

There are three aspects to the view I have just outlined which need to be emphasised separately:

(1)   imagination is the ability to produce ideas which are not memories of impressions;

(2)   the ability is exercised by one's working on one's old ideas;

(3)   what is produced via an exercise of imagination will be an arrangement of ideas one had obtained ultimately through experience, as opposes to pure reflection.

Given that the empiricist view involves (2) and (3) it must hold that saying 'he used his imagination' is a more revealing thing to say than 'he came up with something new', or 'he finished up with something which he did not have before he began to think'. When seen against the background of the empiricist view the comment 'he used his imagination' tells us how it was that he came up with something new; he did so by using his imagination.

Crudely, one can generalise the view that has been presented. It says for any conception, idea, notion, concept one has, which is not something one knows through acquaintance, then it will be produced ultimately by arranging conceptions, ideas, notions, concepts which were gained by acquaintance. Obviously enough, anyone holding this view would see it as playing an explanatory role in giving an account of the creative process in art.

In the history of aesthetics this view has developed important additions. A distinction has been made traditionally between *fancy and imagination*. [17] To use *fancy* as opposed to imagination has either been to combine old ideas in mechanical ways, or in ways which distort reality for fanciful ends. To use imagination has been regarded as involving a more fundamental and inventive shuffling of old ideas, and as producing something which reveals true reality. Art has been regarded as involving imagination, whereas many of those members of the class of which works of art form a sub-class, which are not works of art, have been seen as resulting from the activity of *fancy*.

Very much in terms of this theory art has been coupled with truth, knowledge and faithfulness to reality.[18] On this basis it has been found important to stress the cognitive content of art. To talk as Kant does in the *Critique of Judgement*, imagination, by a dynamical effort, attains the universal or average, which is not simply a mathematical average. Thus, there is the view that in art we confront the universal whatever (man, fear, etc.) which, though it may be seen as a representation of some particular that we know by acquaintance, is nevertheless seen as being true of all particulars of that kind which we do know by acquaintance. This theory can have application even if one considers works of art to be interesting solely because of their formal aspects. One can talk of universal forms.

This view distorts the nature of the creative process. There might be certain truths in the theory, but we must be careful about the way in which they are stated. We need to consider how to describe the relationship between experience and creation.

Consider a primitive case, the kind of case philosophy books so often are concerned with: the conception of the unicorn.[19]

In general form, and in accordance with the empiricist view, it could be held that the conception of the unicorn was achieved by reflection on old ideas. More specifically, and more obviously in empiricist vein, it could be held that the idea of a unicorn is made up out of ideas of properties which do actually exist. However, both the general and specific comments here are troubling. To deal with the specific one first. What is the force of *made up out of*? Does it mean, for example, that the conception of the unicorn involved taking an idea from here, and one from there consciously, and then combining them? If this was the case we might think of coming up with such a conception as analogous to having boxes of coloured bricks such that some arrangements of bricks we had not seen before. Producing a new arrangement of bricks would involve taking a brick from here and one from there, and arranging them: the principle of arrangement could be given, though not the specific application we make of it.

For example,

(1) Aquainted with
$$\begin{array}{|c|} \hline x \\ \hline x \\ \hline \end{array}$$

(2) Acquainted with
$$\begin{array}{|c|} \hline y \\ \hline y \\ \hline \end{array}$$

(3) Acquainted with $\boxed{x}$ $\boxed{x}$ $\boxed{y}$ $\boxed{y}$

(4) Then producing rather than finding $\begin{array}{|c|} \hline x \\ \hline y \\ \hline \end{array}$ where this transcends one's acquaintance.

Here, all we need to provide is x on top of y; we have been given x and y and the notion of *on top of* through x being given on top of x, or y on top of y.

The unicorn, it might be said, is made up of the idea of a horse, the idea of a horn, and the idea of a horn belonging to a head. Making up the conception from these ideas involved holding the ideas before the mind and then combining them.

The following is by no means a fundamental criticism of the above account, but it is something which needs to be understood. It is that even if the conception of the unicorn is arrived at by making it up out of ideas in the way indicated, the ideas held before the mind need not be the ones listed. Fancifully, we might have a number of games all of which permitted one to arrive at an identical situation, though the boxes might contain no identical bits. If arriving at the conception of the unicorn must involve holding ideas before the mind and then shuffling things around a bit, then it is not clear that there are not alternative routes to using the particular ideas horse, horn, horn belongs to head. Further, the ideas which are held before the mind need not in themselves be ideas of particulars or properties which exist. Even in an empiricist account complex ideas not derived directly from experience are possible. The unicorn might be achieved by a conjunction of complex ideas not in themselves derived directly from experience. To admit that creation could be accounted for in this way would not, as such, be to admit an empiricist view. That creation is achieved by holding ideas before the mind and making something new out of them, by rearrangement, is not necessarily empiricist. Empiricism would assert itself by making claims about the ultimate derivation of the ideas involved in the conception of the unicorn. In other words, the empiricist has to claim that the conception of the unicorn ultimately (i.e. sooner or later) involves making up new ideas from ideas derived directly from experience. The move, I have suggested, only delays the point at which one gives the empiricist explanation.

Next, I shall worry about the notion of the unicorn *being made up out of* ideas of states of affairs, observed or learnt about through observation. Why should this notion involve holding the ideas before the mind, and then rearranging them? That is, why should it be interpreted to mean a mental process composed of a number of stages temporally positionable, of which we are conscious, which are analogous to observing the bricks in the various boxes and then moving them? Here, it is well to ask whether the defence of this claim is philosophical or empirical. Empirically it would seem weak. The experience of getting hold of new ideas is not very like the experience which has just been described. The process described is too logical, too deductive, too ordered. This is not to say there could be no such process of discovery, it is only to say it is not characteristic. The artificiality is that of what looks convincingly like a demonstration of how to get there being thought to be convincingly like an account of how we actually do get there.

Consider how we might speak of a contrasting case. A man suddenly thinks of something. It is not for him a given. To think of it is not to remember. For him there is no process of thought which involves holding ideas before the mind and then deriving things from them. The suggestion is that one might suddenly conceive of the unicorn without it being the culmination of a process of thought beginning with the thought of a horse, or whatever.

There are at least three things the empiricist might reply to this.

(1)　There can be no such case.

(2)　This is the case where the discovery is not the result of a conscious process of thought bearing the features exhibited in the other cases, but this does not preclude the discovery being explained by an identical process of thought taking place unconsciously.

(3)　The case can be admitted. Unconscious thought processes do not have to be postulated. The explanation of the perience (i.e. ideas possessed by the thinker). The explanation will always take the form that unless there were some such ideas as these (i.e. ideas derived directly from experience and possessed by the thinker), which the discovery could be indebted to, then it could not be understood how the thinker came to make his discovery.

Neither of the first two replies is worth much. Experience teaches us there are such cases. Unconscious desires and motives are explicable against the backcloth of psychoanalytic theory, but not inoffensive mental processes moving from the horse and horn to the unicorn. Unconscious entities are the kinds of things that we can come to admit we have had all along, although we were not aware of this. For instance, an unconscious desire is the sort of thing we can come to admit as having been there, and as motivating our conduct, though at the time we could not see this. Via psychoanalysis we discover this truth about ourselves. However, it is difficult to see how we could come to the realisation that some while ago one went through a process of thinking (a piece of thinking describable as a temporal sequence) of which one was unconscious at the time. What could ever convince one that some moments ago one held certain ideas before the mind and derived some new idea from them, when one was unaware of doing so at the time. As far as I can see the only thing which might convince one of this, would be the argument that one could not have come up with the new idea unless one had been through such a mental process. The fact that one was unaware of having done so would simply show that the process had been unconscious. However, what is the force of this argument? Why should we accept it? The only respectable notion of the unconscious is that which comes with pyschoanalytic theory. The existence of unconscious processes of thought cannot be guaranteed to take place because they appear to clear up certain areas of philosophical perplexity.

I turn back now to consider the third reply to the case constructed.

Two things to note about the third reply.

Firstly, a point about that aspect of the empiricist view which was given previously as its second aspect. This view is that one's ability to create new things is exercised in holding old ideas before the mind and working upon them. In considering this third reply it is clear that this second aspect of the empiricist view has been dropped. The notion of reflecting on old ideas has nothing to do with this reply: it can, then, be dispensed with.

The second thing about the third reply is this. It conceals a process of thought which is plainly possible. This is not to say that it denies its possibility. What process of thought? The following:

Suppose one has observed and remembers (a) ⬭ (b) ⟳ , and in thinking about (a) and (b) one comes up with ⬔ .

Suppose, coming up with this shape involved thinking that ⬭ was the opposite of ⬭ , and ⬔ was the opposite of ⟳ , and ⬭ could be combined with ⬔ to give ⬔ .

Here the process involved reflecting on old ideas, the end product was derived from them, but the end product cannot properly be said to include the old ideas, or even to be made up to them. The given suggests not a possible rearrangement of itself, but something which does not include itself.

From this consideration, plus previous ones, two claims with consequences for the empiricist case follow. One, creative thought may take place, though conscious reflection on that given directly through experience may not take place. Two, there are cases where reflection on the given can lead to that which does not include the given. In cases such as these what one comes up with does not bear comparison with the notion of a complicated jigsaw, i.e. the notion of a number of bits assembled from a box.

This second claim need not give immediate embarrassment to the kind of empiricist case which is implied by the third reply. Thus, the fact that the ideas given, and reflected on, are not included in the end product is not conclusive against the claim that the end product will be explained by the fact of the thinker having possessed certain ideas which are included in the end product. For instance, though ▭ and ▭▷ are not included in ▭◁< it is true that ▭◁< is made up of, for instance ⌐ , (, < . Thus, it may be maintained, we could not understand how one could create ▭◁< unless there was something given of which the parts of ▭◁< were comprised. Though it is clear that ⌐ , (, < ,were not held before the mind and reflected on, whereas ▭ and ▭▷ were, but were not included, something of the kind ⌐ , (, < ,which is given, is needed to explain ▭◁< .

This is the reply that might be offered, but is it acceptable? The sort of answer, provided by the empiricist account, is that if the thinker is responsible for the end product, then it must fall under descriptions which are within his grasp and which he sees as applying to what he creates. The concepts used, in applying the descriptions, will have been derived from something other than the thinking leading to the creative achievement. Ultimately, it will become apparent that the thinker has those concepts, used in the descriptions, because they have been given in experience. Thus, in terms of the example on hand, it would be pointed out that the thinker would surely see what he had produced as being describable and analysable in terms of concepts like 'lines', 'angles', 'semi-circles', etc., concepts acquired from direct experience of lines, angles and semi-circles. To return to the case of the unicorn: to communicate one's conception, to set it down, might involve describing it. The words used would be words one used prior to the thinking which leads to the unicorn (normally this would be the case). They would be words one could use to refer to those experiences from which they were derived. One sentence one might use in describing the unicorn could be 'it has one horn rising from its forehead'. To be able to handle a sentence like this presupposes having a concept of a horn, of rising, of forehead, etc. The acquisition of concepts is something intimately connected with experience.

However, if the empiricist spells out the presuppositions of creation in this way, it is clear that the empiricist account, as provided earlier, is no longer being advanced. In essence, the view now being expressed is that the creative achievement is a performance of an intelligence which can handle concepts (there must be some way in which the performer can relate, or describe, or perhaps just think his achievement). Conceptual abilities presuppose experience. On this formulation there is no mention of creation involving reflection on old ideas, nor of the end product being made up of the already given, composed of it, being a synthesis of it. There is no longer a theory about the sequence of mental process, and the status of the elements involved in it, a sequence that is, which allows us to come to create things. The thesis has changed to one which cites the origins of an intelligence which can describe and understand what it has done. Therefore, the empiricist has been forced to move from claiming that the product of creative thought is composed of ideas derived directly from experience, to claiming that to think creatively presupposes experience. It is this claim which needs further explanation.

The explanation of the claim that the product of creative thought is composed of ideas derived directly from experience, becomes that what has been achieved will fall under descriptions involving ideas possessed by the creator, which he derived directly from experience. It is entailed, by this view, that the creator can see his product falls under some descriptions using ideas possessed by him prior to his confrontation with the description. However, there are certain kinds of descriptions which, though they involve the appropriate ideas, would not guarantee that the product of creative thought is composed of ideas derived directly from experience. For instance, 'this is a painting using blue, yellow and green pigment'. It is misleading to say that the painting is composed thereby of ideas derived directly from experience. The kind of description with which we must concern ourselves, if trying to substantiate this empiricist thesis, will be as above, e.g. 'it has one horn rising from the forehead'. The kind of descriptions required, in the context of considering works of art and 'entertainment objects', will be fairly specific; they will be descriptions of content, of what the work is about, i.e. 'what's going on in the picture?'—'the dragon is eating a mouse', 'what goes on in the novel?'—'x is shot by y', 'what is going on in the music?'—in this latter case it is more difficult to know what will count as appropriate description.

To pursue the discussion, however, in terms of the primitive case, i.e. the conception of the unicorn.

No doubt, if the thinker was unable to see the applicability of the description about one horn rising from the forehead, he could not be judged to have conceived of the unicorn. If he is deemed to be responsible for the unicorn, he must see the appropriateness of the description. To see the appropriateness of the description entails being able to use its concepts. Typically, the concepts used in the description will be concepts learnt by the thinker rather than invented by him. To speak of learning here, is to speak of concepts acquired directly from experience.

It can be asked whether or not it follows from this that what one comes up with is composed of ideas derived from experience. The procedure, to this point, has been to question the empiricist account until it is seen to withdraw into claims about the necessary origination of descriptions of the conception involved. Now, it is being asked how one moves from these claims about descriptions to the assertion the empiricist must be committed to (i.e. the new being composed of the old).

The empiricist infers from the availability of the description that the experiences upon which the description's availability depends (in some sense of 'depends'), were used in arriving at the new idea. In other stages of the argument the empiricist is likely to use the availability of the description as confirmation of the creative route which his thesis prescribes. However, is our understanding of new situations (for instance, situations we do not create but simply come across) a synthesis of

previous experience, or is previous experience merely a condition of understanding? Thus, how are we to recognise
what's new about what's new? Can it be inferred from the fact
that our understanding of the new issues forth in descriptions
that, therefore, the new can never 'be for us anymore than a
synthesis of previous experience? Such conclusions seem
paradoxical, for what room is left for explanation of original
(including initial) acts of understanding? If we can say we
understand the new because it confronts us as being thus, why
can we not say that we can create the new because of its
possibility?

At this point a positive and contrasting account of creativity
is required. On the critical side it is being urged that the
empiricist-creation theory is an adequate description of creative activity where there is conscious reflection on old ideas,
but that where this is absent then the theory is little better than
a metaphysical prejudice (i.e. similar to the introduction of a
god to explain the origins of the universe). Thus, empiricism
leads in this context to an anti-empiricist posture. Moreover,
not only can it not be inferred from the positive account
offered in the next chapter that the creative process is empiricist (in the sense characterised) but also the availability of the
descriptions discussed is shown to be open to a very different
interpretation, namely that any state of affairs would fall
under descriptions within our conceptual system, because
that system contains the logical limits of possibility. Anything,
therefore, falls within it. Here, we have the difference
between a move in chess and completing a piece of the jigsaw.
The completed piece is a synthesis of some of the pieces in the
puzzle, whereas a brilliant move by Fischer is incorrectly
understood if seen as a mere synthesis of some of the rules of
chess, though the brilliant move will fall within those rules and
will be describable in terms of them.

3
Creativity and 'as ifness'

What, then, do we do when confronted with the apparently legitimate question about the origination of an 'entertainment object' and the process of thought which leads to its completion? We can begin to approach these unanswered questions if the question of the intentionality of creativity is looked into first. In thinking about this we learn more about the context in which creative thought takes place. (As a word of warning, it is worth saying that many of the wrong questions occur, and the wrong emphases are put, if one fails to attend to what it is like to create something. It is easy to blunder into questions which fail to catch the activity involved.) For those who know about the 'intentional fallacy' problem in contemporary aesthetics,[20] it will be seen that the thesis to be outlined almost goes against the presupposition that there *are* intentions which may or may not be relevant to the critical enquiry.

Suppose it is insisted that if original, a work of art or an 'as if' object must be the result of creative activity and that, in some sense, that which is the result of creative activity will not be covered by intentions. It need not follow that creative activity is unintentional, an accident, the result of random activity, for we might maintain the creative achievement is non-intentional. We might insist that the production of things and events by intelligent beings can either be explained by intention, accident, or creative activity. That explaining something by reference to a creative act gives us a distinct kind of explanation we might bring out in the following way. Our notion of intention presupposes the possibility of failing to execute our intentions; thus a man would not be telling us what his intentions were if we knew there was no logical possibility of his failing to execute them. With this established, we might argue that if a line in a poem constitutes the result of executing an intention, then it cannot be that the intention executed was one which, prior to its execution, could have been stated in the form 'I intend to make up the

42

line ....'. In the light of this logical stricture about intention, we might conclude that whereas knowing what action I am going to perform is a necessary condition of performing an intentional action, knowing which line I am going to make up is a sufficient condition of not being able to have an intention to make up that line. The whole point, of course, is that one can never be in the position of knowing which line it is that one is going to make up. It makes no sense to speak of the prior knowledge of the full result of a creative act; to have full knowledge of the creative act guarantees that it has been performed. 'Creative act' may seem too generous a description here since much of our on-going thinking would be covered by the same point; however, the point does cover creative activity.

To go on from this to claim that works of art or 'as if' objects are not covered by intentions is quite inadequate. It surely makes sense to say 'he intends to write a poem about love', 'he intends to paint a brighter picture next time', 'he intends to put green paint there', 'he intends to write a symphony', 'he intends to write a novel in the style of Gertrude Stein'. Such statements of intention are very general, and to know they were executed would be to be in a position to offer only very bare descriptions of the work produced. However, it is possible to think of statements of intention which are more specific, which point more directly to the characteristic achievements of the work. For instance, 'I intend to change him into someone more sympathetic', 'I intend to make him give her the ring', 'I intend to paint a dazzling golden star in the middle of the sky'. One can say one intended to come up with a certain idea, which one did in fact come up with, in so far as one intended to find something that would fit in with other things, and the idea one had did fit in. This might be thought analogous to trying to find the bit of stone which has the right shape for fitting into one's mosaic, but the analogy is not complete. In the latter case, one can know just which shaped-piece it is that will fit in yet still possess an unexecuted intention, whereas in the former case this is not possible. Typically, creative acts will be performed as a response to some or many intentions one has. Thus, an incident in a novel's sixth chapter may answer the intention to write a novel, the intention to fill it with the macabre and the grotesque, the intention to make it reach a satisfactory climax. To reiterate a point already made, the creative act when performed, no matter what its context, no matter how related to an intention, must always fall under some description which could not have been used in stating the initial intention.

Incidentally, we may note that we have uncovered the basis of an argument against determinism. It is a tenet of the determinist case that any piece of human behaviour, thought, action, etc., could be predicted prior to its occurrence. The thesis is, if we knew enough this would be so, or this would be possible. Now, if we confine our attention to those events of a new kind which are creative acts, then it becomes clear that we will never be able to predict that a new kind of creative act (of such and such a nature) will occur sooner or later. The reason for this is that one will have to perform the creative act in question in order to give some semblance of having made the prediction about it. In other words, within the species there can be no predicting the creative acts of the species as a whole.

At this point we can ask the questions, 'how is it one gets the ideas one comes up with?', and 'how are creative acts possible?' The general answer is to point to how particular ideas, how particular creative acts, are arrived at. Normally, they are not isolated things but integral to the whole process, the whole enterprise. The creator is involved in a piece of thinking and judging which must go beyond his anticipations; he must know he cannot have anything like full anticipations in this area. One can anticipate, as one sets out to create a work, that one will often not know what one is going onto, and often one will not know how to go on. As one gets into the creative process one's ideas will be related to those which have gone before; often they will be related as answers to problems. They will constitute answers to the creator's constant question 'given all of this, what will happen next?' 'What shall I do next?' How they occur, how they are possible, is seen by looking at the specific problems, the specific contexts in which they arose. They were possible in the light of everything else that was done, they manifest the creator's ability to find the right thing. He has this ability in so far as he can see something is required, and can provide it. It is misleading to suggest that he finds it as the collector finds lepidoptera. We do say 'then I found the right idea', but we should not mean this in the sense that the idea was somewhere (perhaps in fragmentary form) and one finds it, picks it up (puts it together) and finally fits it into its niche. The creative act is the way in which thinking of a certain kind is continued or sustained. It is neither helpful nor explanatory to try to break the performance down into one dealing with materials which, in themselves, have nothing to do with the particular work which is being created. The situation created suggests possibilities to the creator. These possibilities will constitute developments of what is already there, or compliments or contrasts. Here we might compare seeing the possibilities with seeing a new situation. As a matter of fact we can see what is new about new situations. The new object we encounter around the corner we treat as the unique particular that it is. The fact that we will describe it by using the language we already possess does not automatically point to our dealing with it by seeing how it is composed of old situations we have witnessed. Our ability to describe it might be explained by arguing that our language must be applicable necessarily to all possible worlds. To think as we do think is to be able to think about, and therein make sense of, any situation which confronts us. In the creative process what we eventually come up with is the new situation; it will be something we have made rather than something we discover and begin observing.

One explains how the thought is arrived at by pointing to the train of thoughts of which it forms part. One indicates that it is the right bit for there. Suddenly the creator sees what he could not see before. He brings himself to his own kind of discovery by engaging in sustained thinking of the appropriate kind. What I am trying to suggest is that it will be the complexity of the created thing that points to greater complexity, and suggests the possibility of new departures. It is also at this point that the enterprise gains in difficulty. One may be agonised looking for the idea with which to begin, but it is only later that one can make big mistakes; one does this by failing, in subsequent moves, to hold all of the ends together, or by failing to let go of some and missing a simplification.

At this point it might be thought the swing of the argument against an empiricist conception of creativity has gone too far. Creative activity might now seem a set of isolated episodes, instead of something which depends upon a whole person and a particular culture, plus its traditions. If the emphasis has gone too far then it must be corrected. It has been one of the great features of modern scholarship that we have asserted the history of our creative achievements[21] and this must be heeded. Similarly, it must be affirmed that abilities are acquired in experience and develop through experience. Thus, that Poussin painted as he did and not like Picasso was not a matter of personal choice, and that Dürer's hand was extraordinarily accurate was a skill he developed through experience. What is being argued, on the other side, is that it is simply because possibilities are possibilities, and solutions to problems are solutions to problems that we have the capacity to arrive at them. Thus, seeing 4 as the sum of $2 + 2$ is explained by 4 being the sum of $2 + 2$. It is not as though the gap between seeing and not seeing that 4 is the sum of $2 + 2$ is filled by some unconscious process of deduction. Even the most vigorous stream of deductive thought is full of steps where one is called to see that something is the case, and one does see it because it is. What I am denying sense to is the notion which, according to L.L. Whyte in his book *The Unconscious Before Freud,*[22] has been gathering increased momentum ever since Descartes severed mind from body and identified thought with that of which we are conscious. Pre-Freudian, and for that matter post-Freudian theories of the unconscious have used this concept as a way of introducing a mysterious element into any account of creative activity, and yet one of the principal motives behind this has depended upon an insistence on mechanical explanations. Basically, it has been thought that as we often find ourselves suddenly with the solution to some problem (perhaps after looking for it for days) then there must be some process of thought which led to it. However, as consciousness makes no report of this process it is assumed it did take place, though eluding consciousness. With this apparently established the theories tend to become rhapsodic or poetic. Consciousness, we are told, is the mere tip of the iceberg, whereas the real depth of mind lies beneath the surface. It is from these depths that inspiration and our great powers spring, and all of this is concealed from the 'natural light of reason'. If, however, one goes on to worry about what happens when, beneath the surface of the mind, we are creative, the theories tend to leave us with nothing better than an empiricist theory of creativity. In other words, accumulations of experience undergo unconscious assembly; something takes place and it is something we miss; we find ourselves the inheritors from a benefactor with whom we have no direct acquaintance.

Of course, not all thoughts of possibilities are equally possible at all times, but on the other side the difference between contemporaries who see the possibilities and others who fail is hardly explicable by reference to differing sets of experiences. In an account of creativity, full room must be left for the influential solution (including influential near misses), the capacity for thinking it, and the species' persistence as a whole (meaning that solutions are arrived at similarly, in some ways, to a nest of wasps finding the jampot; the persistence of the nest leads one of its members to the pot and subsequently, therefore, the rest).

The empiricist-creation theory is a theory about a faculty or function of the mind. It is alleged this faculty or function constitutes our creativity. At this point in the enquiry it may be asked if there *are* any general functions of mind which our creativity presupposes. It has been argued that creating music presupposes the activity of imagining as the mode in which creative thought occurs, but this is a presupposition governing a particular instance, whereas what is now required are the presuppositions, or rather (anticipating the outcome) the presupposition, governing creativity in general. The feature of consciousness which satisfies this enquiry is one without which human consciousness could not be. It is a feature detailed by Sartre, especially in *L'Imaginaire*.[23]

Human thought is not confined to present sensations and perceptions. It ranges over the past, absent phenomena of the present, the future, the possible and the impossible. Without this ability there would be none of the creative activities I have been describing. We can think of what is not present, of that which has no being; if you like, human consciousness originates a realm of nothingness. The other side of this ability is our being able to think of what is present; we are not overwhelmed by what is presented, we attend to our consciousness of it and thereby direct consciousness to it. It is this which is so distinctive of human consciousness. In its creative role human consciousness gives content to 'not being'. Works of art and 'entertainment objects' remain obstinately constituents of 'not being', although this may seem paradoxical for certainly they exist. In saying they are constituents of 'not being' no more is meant than saying they are necessarily constituents of an 'as if' world, but what this means it is the purpose of subsequent chapters to reveal. What needs to be said now is that the possibility of the 'as if' depends upon our ability (in thought) to negate being.

The other side of this enquiry, which requires general clarification, is the negated being or, and more particularly and more relevantly for the purposes of this book its 'as if' manifestations. Chapter 1 provided a possible, concrete example of the 'as if', and several subsequent chapters will be concerned to demonstrate the necessary 'as if' character of a range of our art forms, but what is required at present is some general grasp of the structure of 'as ifness'.

Although such expressions as 'as if' situation, 'as if' object 'as if' experience have no conventionally established position within the language, they are not meant as technical concepts or idiosyncratic to the present work. For instance, to have an 'as if' experience is for it to have been *as if* one had such and such an experience. The second 'as if' in the last sentence is one we all understand. It is, then, to our general awareness of 'as ifness' that I wish to draw attention. We speak of what I am calling the 'as if' when we use expressions like 'x only seems to be y', 'x only appears to by y', 'x is as if it is y', 'x looks like y', 'x only looks to be y'. Thus, what I call an 'as if' object or situation or experience are objects. situations, experiences describable by means of these expressions. The concepts listed, which explicate the sphere of the 'as if', are very general in their applications. We have more specific concepts than these as will be seen in looking at the various 'as if' characterisations of different art forms in subsequent chapters. Generally, the more specific notions can be reduced to the notions already indicated.

'As ifness' is the sphere of likeness where likeness involves the possibility of something being taken for something else. In other words it is not the notion of likeness involved in saying a circle is like a square in so far as both are geometrical figures. 'As ifness' is the situation where one thing seems to be something else, where it is as if it is. This general area is divided in some important ways for the purpose of this book. There are those situations where taking one thing for another or thinking of one as the other is delusive and there are those situations where, for various reasons, there is no delusion but where taking one thing for another is the way one apprehends the situation. Cutting across this distinction is the distinction between voluntary and compulsive experiences, and also a distinction between verisimilitude and inferential similarity. Many 'as if' situations are designed to be so and they are responded to in knowledge of the design and in accordance with it. For instance, x's death in a play is a situation in which actors design a series of actions so that they will be taken for the death of x, where there is in fact no such death. The fact that the one situation is not the other is fairly obviously an important dimension of the 'as if'. The social and institutional set up, in this sort of case, is just that the one situation be read as the other in full knowledge that it is not the other. For the audience the experience is, because of the established conventions governing the case, compulsive. There are some other cases where delusion is ruled out and where the experience is compulsive but where design is not present. Such a case is the mirror image, or, because mirrors themselves are designed to reflect, reflections in general. More generally well-known illusions constitute similar cases. Instances of this kind, including both designed and natural cases, are not transparently what they are and therefore there is no guarantee of them not being delusive. However, such possibilities are rare (has anyone ever been in the position of Narcissus) and the general experience is one of knowingly being captivated in contemplating the way something only seems. Situations of this general kind I will call *magnetic* or *hypnotic* 'as if' situations, and they constitute the main subject matter of several following chapters. In terms of traditional aesthetics this theme is one of mimesis or the representational properties of art objects. Our imaginings also fit into the general characterisation which has been offered. In general they do not delude, yet a sequence of thoughts and experiences are taken as being other than they are, thus the seeming to see palm trees of the fantasy, tropical island is thought of as seeing the palm trees. Moreover, the experience is quite compulsive, not in the sense that it deludes, but in so far as seeming to see has to be thought of as seeing, despite the knowledge that it is only seeming to see. What needs to be remarked on, in these situations, is that the likenesses involved are not ponderously ascertained; in fact the judgment of likeness is retrospectively appropriate following the magnetic attraction. A clear example of this is coming to see a reflection having had at first some difficulty in doing so. One does not match up the reflection slowly against what it is a reflection of, as one might check through a suspect banknote to see if it is genuine. One moment one does not see it, the next one does, it is then, realising that it is only, for example, water at which one is looking, that one can reflect on one state of affairs being like another. In the case of imagining it is not even as though there is some material (as there is water in the reflection case) which can be identified independently of what seems to be the case and about which questions of likeness can be asked. Certainly patterns of electrical activity in the brain would be unlikely candidates. The recognition of seeming to see comes from the experience of a seeing which is not a seeing.

The magnetic 'as if' situation does not exhaust the 'as if' sphere. There are many situations where an awareness of likeness between two states of affairs gives one the choice of seeing one as the other. For instance, the death of x may resemble the death of y and because of this one may allow oneself the indulgence of perceiving it as if it was y's death. This case is very different from that of x's death in the play. Added to these sorts of cases are those where one thinks of one state of affairs as another on the basis of delusion or, more simply, mistake. For instance, where a judgment of particular identity is called for and where one mistakes the copy for the original. The whole experience in this kind of case is one of it being as if one was perusing the original. The 'as ifness' drops out when the mistake is rectified. When this is so one is left with a mere copy. This example is not *magnetic* because it cannot survive the revelation. Where we know that x is not the original (y) but a copy, then it stands on its own feet as the same kind of thing as y, something to be taken on for what it is in itself; there is nothing that can make it seem as if it is y except for misleading surroundings (which put us back in the position of not knowing it is the copy). Cases of the kind I have been considering in this paragraph I will call *neutral 'as if situations*. They have no real significance for my purposes, although some of the cases involve the magnetic 'as if' through their dependence upon *imaginings*. Thus, the way the second death becomes as if it was the first is through imagining it as though it was, although that it is readily imaginable is dependent upon the one death being like the other. Another possible *neutral* 'as if' situation is where similar evidence gives rise to the inference that a certain state of affairs is so, when it is not. For instance, to the listener at home, music playing in place of the Test match commentary may make it seem as if bad weather has stopped play, whereas, in reality, radio contact between the ground and the broadcasting authority may have been lost. As with the case of the copy and original the discovery of the facts of the case destroy the 'as if' interpretation. It is no longer as if it is raining at the Test match when you know that music replaces the commentary because of lost radio contact.

That one state of affairs can be taken as another, so that it is as if it is the other, is, apart from the cases of imagining things, heavily context-dependent. This is fairly obviously the case where similarity in evidence leads to an incorrect inference and where the 'as if ' attribution is post-correction and past tense, but the same is true of magnetic 'as if' situations as well. The perception of a picture, for example, is heavily dependent upon learning about pictorial conventions. The hypnotic characteristics of 'as if' situations result from compelling likeness, but that there is this likeness depends upon an involved interaction of circumstances. Without knowing something of the context it is possible for any situation to be taken for any other situation, although given the specification of a context, and from the point of view of that context, certain situations can seem as others and others cannot. The compelling quality of the likeness in the *magnetic situation*, a feature which survives any discovery of unlikeness (the discovery that one situation is not the other) is not only context dependent, but dependent upon the likeness-relation being between radically different kinds of things. There is nothing remarkable in two things of the same kind being so much alike as to be identical, for example two taps. In a sense, the point is why should they not be? In such a case one needs very special circumstances for being able to think of one as the other (e.g. someone trying to deceive one). The situation with things of different kinds is quite different. Consider the case of the tap and the hologram of the tap. The point is how can something which is so obviously not a tap seem so much like one? What is interesting here, which the previous question points to, is that the hologram of a tap seems to be a tap (and *only* seems to be one) whether or not there is a particular tap with which it might be confused and whether or not any taps exist. For a particular tap, whether there are other taps or not, it cannot seem to be a tap (unless one can rig up some special context where it seems to be a hologram and thus is experienced as seeming to be a tap); a real tap has to be a tap, though it can seem to be a particular one which it is not. Of course special circumstances are required for one to attend to the hologramic properties of the hologram. For instance, in the similar case of reflections on the surface of water, the threat of drowning is likely to remove in one an interest in the surface reflections. In other words the *magnetism*, though compelling, is resistible. In the case of imagining, the feature of radically different kinds of things as a feature of magnetic 'as if' situations reappears in that one's thoughts are of a radically different kind when they lack, what we may call, a real object. It is just as curious and interesting to reflect on how thought, which structurally seems to have real objects, can sustain itself despite not having real objects, as it is to reflect on how something of one kind can appear so like something of another kind. The notion of thought and the absence or presence of real objects is a little rough and ready for describing the variety of situations imagining encompasses. Covered are those situations in which one imagines fairies, but not so clearly covered is, say, imagining the past behaviour of a friend. Perhaps the general point is better covered by means of a particular sort of case which avoids talk or real objects. Thus, there are certain experiences we have which are like seeing things but which are only seeming to see things. This sort of experience is typical of imagining where the reality or unreality of what one is imagining is cut across by the unreality written into the experiencing of it. Seeming to see something (in the case of intentional imagining as opposed to the case of perceptual mistake) is an experience different in kind from actually seeing something. Seeming to see something is not a kind of seeing.[24] The interesting fact is that one experience, different in kind from another and known to be, can nonetheless masquerade as the other. Put round the other way, one experience can masquerade as the other, where it is known not to be the other, just because it is of a different kind but like the other. It is possible to extrapolate from the general features of this kind of case to see on what basis fiction, which is to be read, works. It works by inducing experiences that are like but of a different kind from others, but which are thought of *as* those others. In the case of pictures, on the other hand, it is not verisimilitude in terms of kinds of experience which is aimed at but verisimilitude *vis-à-vis* what the experience is an experience of.

There is a work by Vaihinger called *The Philosophy of 'As if*[25] which it might seem should be turned to in considering the general structure of 'as ifness'. The obligation is one of relating one's own work to the history of the subject. However, in this particular case there is no real history of the subject (or certainly so in terms of the subject being considered generally) apart from the prima facie relevant work by Vaihinger, and on analysis this work proves to be without actual relevance. Vaihinger's interests lie within epistemology. His concern with the 'as if' is in terms of the utility of thinking of something as if it was something else when knowing that it is not, or being sceptical of it. The basic ideas in Vaihinger seem to be that absolute knowledge is impossible, that thought proceeds by means of comparison and that an apparently falsified hypothesis can, as fiction, be useful. His philosophy is a strange blending of Kantian and positivist elements, yielding a position describable as idealist positivism. Fictions which have no utility, in the sense of producing perceptions of the universe as ordered and unified, are thought of as merely fanciful, and not what Vaihinger is recommending. Therefore, mere magnetic 'as ifness' is not at the centre of Vaihinger's interest; it is not this which is his subject. His interest is in things like thinking of matter as if it is composed of atoms, thinking of the universe as if it had a creator. Out of such suppositions (even if false and known to be) a certain comfort is derived and some extensions of knowledge become possible. However, this notion of the 'as if ' is far removed from the notion I have been discussing. To entreat 'let us think of x as if it is y' is to offer an instruction with which one could comply, despite it being the case that it is not that x *is* as if it is y. For instance, one can think of the circulation of the blood as if it was a road transportation system. The arteries constitute the motorways and major roads, the veins and capillaries the minor road network. To engage in this supposition might prove instructive in so far as one might come to certain realisations about blood circulation that had not previously been possible. This is not to say though that the circulatory blood system appears as if it is a road network, as if one might mistake it for one. To think of one thing in terms of something else is not to say that it is as if it is that something else. Vaihinger's interest in thinking of one thing as if it is something else is no more than the interest of thinking of one thing in terms of something else (thinking of it in terms of an analogous case). In which case my interest in the 'as if' can be sharply differentiated from Vaihinger's: in fact we are not discussing the same concept.

With some grasp both of the kind of consciousness required for the 'as if' and the general structure of 'as ifness' itself, it is now possible to proceed to consider how basic the notion is to an understanding of what society considers its art forms. Several following chapters will be concerned with this project.

4

Drama and the 'as if'

It might be said of Hamlet that 'he seems to lack the capacity for action', of a character in a Maigret novel that 'he seems guilty', of certain happenings in *The Turn of the Screw* that 'they seem fantastic', all of which we might say of real people and real happenings. Further, the evidence and reasons by which we decide of actual people and incidents that they have capacities for action, that they are guilty, that they are fantastic, must not differ in kind from the evidence and reasons we cite when making judgments about the Prince of Denmark, etc. Thus, that which would not count as sufficient evidence for an actual person's incapacity for action, for example, hatred of an uncle, cannot count as evidence for Hamlet's incapacity for action. This is not to overlook the nature of certain predictions which are based on the knowledge of a literary form. For instance, that character x in the detective story has done nothing suspicious might be good grounds for believing him guilty of the murder, because we know this is usually the case in detective stories. Thus, knowledge of detective-story procedure, where the apparently innocent are so often the guilty, would be no grounds for suspecting a real man. However, none of this denies that one's guilt is not established by those features which point to one's innocence, whether or not the context is fictional.

These judgments using the verb 'to seem' which are about the content of a work do not preclude more authoritative judgments. It may be true that Hamlet lacks the capacity for action, that some of the happenings in *The Turn of the Screw* are fantastic etc. Despite this, in the case of the theatre at least, I think the following true: descriptions of the content of a work must fall within brackets which are governed by an 'as if ' consideration. For example, though it is true that the character Hamlet lacks the capacity for action, it is nevertheless true that it only seems to be the case that there is a Hamlet who lacks the capacity for action. Further, though it might be

55

true of the content of a work that it only seems to be the case that there is an x who kills y, it will nevertheless be true that it only seems to be the case that it only seems to be the case that there is an x who kills y. The same point can be made, in a more concrete way, by stressing that if the stage action took place, and the actors did not have to make out that they were other than they were, then, whatever it was that confronted the audience, it would not be theatre, or drama, or a play or acting. The important thing about the theatre is that what goes on falls within a bracket governed by an 'as if' consideration. The actor engages in a form of pretence, thus acting is pretending within the context of the theatre. These facts are primitive facts about the nature of drama, and although they are not over-informative they can be overlooked. It is my argument that facts such as these are primitive facts about the accredited art forms, and to emphasise this I will examine possible criticisms, as well as try to demonstrate such facts are present in areas where they are concealed. In the theatre that pretence characterises the theatrical situation, and that 'pretence' is a concept belonging within the 'as if ' may seem unalarming, yet the position is not without critics. In philosophical terms, an involved criticism is one very much implied by Austin's 1957-8 article on pretending.[26] No doubt, Austin would have wanted to distinguish between 'pretending' and the various concepts of dramatic representation, however, as I do not want to do this I interpret Austin's article as a criticism of the way in which I have characterised theatre.

In summary form, Austin's argument has in design the role of combating the view that pretending is 'identical with being (or being doing) except that some special feature is left out', and it yields the analysis, 'to be pretending in the basic case, I must be trying to make others believe or to give them the impression, by means of a current personal performance in their presence, that I am (really, only, etc.) abc, in order to disguise the fact that I am really xyz.'

It is a consequence of the view Austin attacks, that to pretend, or to be pretending to be or to do, entails not really nor actually being, or not really nor actually doing. That this is a consequence of the view Austin attacks can be brought out in the following way: one might hold the very general view that in being and doing there is always some special feature (what feature it is may vary from case to case but it will always be special) which must be present, and, if present, then necessarily one is or is doing, and that such features are absent when one pretends, or is pretending to be or to do. Add to this view, another view, namely a sufficient condition of not really being or not really doing is the absence of such special features, and the consequence mentioned follows. Of course, this latter view ('a sufficient condition of not really being or not really doing is the absence of such special features') commits one to the misleading view that the boxer who goes fifteen rounds with his opponent did not really knock his opponent out, and commits one to this in virtue of the fact that going fifteen rounds with an opponent precludes having had one's opponent counted out. Possibly the difficulty is removed if one adds to the general view indicated, the view that given what one is or is doing bears a distinct ressemblance to what one might be or might be doing, then the absence of such special features entails not really being or not really doing.

It is difficult to see how this general thesis can be made plausible without reducing it to its consequence, and I take it as being at least an even bet that those who have not reflected on these issues would accept the truth of the consequence. What is true is that Bedford[27] (Austin's opponent in this discussion) provides a case which, if he was correct in what he said about it, would not disconfirm the thesis. If it is legitimate to generalise Bedford's argument, the generalisation would be that where to do x is to be y, then in pretending to be y to do x is to cease pretending to be y, and that for any *being y* there is some doing x which is so related to it. Given that this generalisation was true one would not have substantiated the general thesis, but would have shown that it applied to all cases of pretending to be. However, the example which Bedford gave upon which I have based the generalisation is too flimsy to bear its bulk. As Austin interprets Bedford, Bedford is advising us to disbelieve the man, whom we discover smashing up the furniture in our home, when he tells us he is pretending to be angry, moreover, not only must we disbelieve him, but we must conclude that he is angry. Austin fells this account with one neat punch: 'here surely Mr Bedford carries the philosopher's professional addiction to furniture to a new pitch of positive concern for it.'

It is compatible with, and I think required by the consequence of this general thesis, i.e. 'to pretend or to be pretending to be or to do entails not really nor actually being, or not really nor actually doing', that either some feature(s) of really or actually being, or of really or actually doing must be absent, or some feature(s) incompatible with really or actually being or really or actually doing must be present. However, this is not to speak of special features, special in the sense that whenever the feature(s) then the being or doing, and whenever the being or doing then the feature(s).

For Austin, it is a necessary condition of pretending that one disguises or deceives as to how one really is, or as to what one really is doing, by some piece of contemporary behaviour. That which conceals is 'genuine behaviour simulated', that which is concealed is 'real behaviour dissembled'. That, in certain cases, the contemporary behaviour does disguise, or deceive, depends upon it being taken as evidence for one's being in a certain state of mind; one's pretence in this sort of case will most definitely be pretending to be x, and may involve pretending to y, and presumably will involve pretending to do something x-ily. This analysis has the consequence that in many cases of pretending what one pretends will not really be the case. Thus, where what one pretends to be or to do conceals the fact one is not, or is not doing what one pretends, then obviously enough what one pretends to be or to do will not really be the case; I cannot conceal the fact that I did not kick you, if in pretending to kick you I really did kick you. In such cases to really do what one pretends to do entails a contradiction, for there is nothing concealed, and to conceal is, for Austin, the essence of pretence. In terms of intentions the thesis must be that what distinguishes pretending to be or to do from being or doing is the intention to conceal, or to disguise; a matter of, as the quotation I gave from Austin at the outset suggests, trying to make others believe something, or trying to give them a convincing impression of something. Such an intention is not only the essence of the situation in pretending, or a necessary condition of pretending, but also it allows Austin to hold that that which conceals may be that which one really does or is, though it is what one pretends to do or be, and thus may be fully intentional. Austin's thesis denies, then, the consequence of the general thesis discussed, and yet, at the same time, shows why a great number of examples we might choose to investigate appear to conform to the view that what is being pretended is not the case.

If Austin's analysis is found in any way obscure it can be clarified by discussing two examples, which he himself chooses to discuss. Magicians pretend to saw ladies in half; the whole point of the act is to make it look as if the lady is being sawn in half when she is not. Thus, genuine behaviour simulated, i.e. sawing her in half, disguises real behaviour dissembled, i.e. not sawing her in half. The genuine behaviour simulated is that which the magician pretends to do, and of course in such a case he cannot do what he pretends to do, for then there would be nothing to disguise, nothing to conceal; to saw the lady in half is to have given up pretending, it becomes 'a grim reality'. According to Austin, although the magician does not do what he pretends to do, this is not explained by the general rule pretending to do=not doing; there is, however, supposed to be a rule involved, and what rule it is can be brought out in considering another example. A thief disguises himself as a window-cleaner, and pretends to be cleaning windows in order to note valuables, which can be seen through the window. The whole point of what the thief pretends is to conceal or disguise his real purpose, or what he is really up to. The genuine behaviour simulated, i.e. cleaning the windows, disguises real behaviour dissembled, i.e. noting the valuables. The genuine behaviour simulated is that which the thief pretends to be doing, and of course (and this 'of course' is Austin's) he can do what he pretends to do, or he can be doing what he pretends to be doing, for, even if he is doing it, he is still concealing something. In such a case then, pretending to do, or be doing =not doing (i.e. a supposed general rule) does not work, but a rule, which works for both cases, is that genuine behaviour simulated must conceal, and thus must not in its execution make it such that there is nothing to conceal. This is Austin's position.

Within the pretence situation some behaviour, or the performance of some actions, is required. This is not true of pretending to oneself, but as this is a case Austin declines to discuss we may put it to one side. To say the pretence situation requires the performance of some actions is to say that it requires that certain things are really done. The distinction between really doing a thing and not really doing a thing is exemplified when we consider the magician's sawing and the surgeon's sawing. Of course, pretending to do is, as Austin points out, as good an example of an action as any other, but what is required in the pretence situation is some doing which is other than pretending to do, or, and perhaps more accurately, some doing which falls under descriptions which do not entail that one is pretending to do. Thus, when I pretend to kick you, I kick, I miss you by an inch, etc., or when the magician pretends to saw the lady in half, he moves the saw to and fro, and bends his back. Pretending, then, requires behaviour which falls under descriptions which do not entail that one is pretending. For Austin there is in the pretence situation some real behaviour dissembled, some genuine behaviour simulated, and some other behaviour, pretence behaviour, which includes but is not exhausted by the act of pretending. With these distinctions established Austin states his thesis. The thesis is that it does not much matter if the pretence behaviour coincides with the genuine behaviour simulated as long as the contrast is preserved between genuine behaviour simulated and real behaviour dissembled. In so far as the genuine behaviour simulated must not coincide with real behaviour dissembled, nor be equivalent to the very reverse of the real behaviour dissembled, it is entailed that one's pretence behaviour, in pretending, must not coincide with the behaviour one is concealing, because then the behaviour is not being concealed, and also that the pretence behaviour must not be the very reverse of the behaviour to be concealed, because then there would be nothing to conceal. This is Austin's analysis.

What then, from my point of view, is wrong with this analysis?

If Austin holds that there are cases (or there can be cases) in which what one pretends disguises, then we may ask how does one decide that these are cases of pretending? If, for example, we answered that where what one pretends disguises then there we decide that what disguises is being pretended by ascertaining that it is something which is disguising, then this would leave us with a very queer state of affairs. But it is not clear that Austin leaves us with any more than a somewhat modified queer state of affairs of this order. If we hold that to ascertain that something disguises is to have ascertained that that something is being pretended, then we must argue that pretending to do x is what one pretends, in the sense that one pretends to pretend to do x, and that everything which one does in order to pretend (where what one does in order to pretend disguises) is what one pretends. Of course, Austin does not wish to say anything as silly as this, but this does not indicate how he is to be saved from this charge.

It is true that Austin holds the element of disguise in pretence is a necessary and not a sufficient condition of pretence, it is also true that in the situation in which one is, or does, what one pretends to be or do Austin must hold that a necessary condition of so pretending is intending what one pretends as a disguise. We may now consider two quite separate questions.

(1) If by y I am disguising x am I thereby pretending?
(2) If by y I am disguising x am I thereby pretending to do y?

Austin's answer to the first question is that I am not, thus disguise is a necessary and not a sufficient condition of pretending. A negative answer to the first question entails a negative answer to the second. Further features of the pretence situation for Austin are (i) the one who pretends must remain on the scene, and (ii) in terms of intentions one must either be intending to deceive or intending to give a convincing impression. We can see then why Austin does not think the fact of x disguising y guarantees a pretence. It is still clear, however, that we pretend to be or to do all sorts of things which we never suspected we pretend to be or to do. The schoolboy in refraining from opening his mouth (such that the sweet will not be observed) is pretending to refrain from opening his mouth, the magician is pretending to move the saw to and fro, the demonstration of mock anger in stamping the foot and biting the carpet involves one in both pretending to stamp one's foot and bite the carpet. Obviously something has gone wrong. The thief is applying his cloth to the window, yet this is compatible with his pretending to be cleaning windows. Why is it, in this case, pretending to be cleaning the windows, whereas in the other cases, not pretending to be refraining from opening one's mouth, etc? Surely, if the thief is really cleaning the windows then he is not pretending to be cleaning them, though he may be pretending to be a window-cleaner and even pretending that cleaning windows is all he is about. Similarly, on the stage an actor who eats a banana sandwich does not pretend to eat it, though he may be pretending to be a man eating a banana sandwich out of politeness. Austin's analysis cannot be sustained, and even if it could be it would not be a fundamental attack on the 'as if' status of pretence. For Austin, though pretending to do does not entail not doing, one has to make it seem as if one is not something that, of course, despite the seeming, one has to be. The opposite side of this is one of making it seem as if one is wholly or exclusively something other than what one is making it seem one is not. The behaviour then is still very much an 'as if' phenomenon.

A neater challenge to the rule that pretending to do or to be = not doing or not being is provided by Miss Anscombe in the form of a counterexample.[28] She points out, quite correctly, that one could pretend to be poisoned when one was in a situation where one did not know one was. Therefore, a lack of knowledge allows one to pretend to be what one is. This possibility is not confined to states of oneself, for institutional facts create the same possibility. For instance, in a pantomime the prince, who has has his identity concealed from himself, may pretend to be the prince. However, that the general rule fails is so only because of the generality or lack of specificity of 'pretending to be x'. To explain: pretending to be poisoned when one is will involve behaviour like simulating paroxysms of pain when there is no pain, and pretending to be the prince, when one does not know one is, will involve behaviour like simulating regal confidence when one is ultra nervous. In other words, to pretend to be x when one is will only be possible in so far as one is pretending to be y or doing y when not y nor doing y. What one is pretending to be, or be doing, which one is not, nor doing, will be what one's pretending to be, when one is, reduces to; pretending to be poisoned will be a general way of referring to one's pretending to be in an agonised, poisoned state, which one is not.

As acting is a form of pretending, albeit a highly specialised form of pretending, then from the preceding considerations it can be seen how theatre is an 'as if' phenomenon. Contemporary developments in theatre might seem to run counter to this characterisation but on analysis I do not think they do. Particularly, for example, the developments in theatre covered in Ansorge's book *Disrupting the Spectacle* (especially the chapter entitled: Games People Play).[29] What I am arguing for is a very primitive and basic fact about theatre, and one which is not fundamentally challenged by the destruction of the rigorous blueprint (the play), the incorporation of improvisation, the obliteration of the distinction between actor and audience or the advent of politically motivated street-theatre. *Avant-garde* theatre has very much attacked the theatre of deception and illusion, and claims to produce theatrical experience which is real. However, *avant-garde* theatre has not been as philosophically motivated as the terms of the discussion sometimes suggest, and in fact its attack has been directed at much more substantial opponents. In particular it has tried to offer an alternative to bourgeois theatre. It has denigrated the notion of the 'great work' to be performed by the 'great actors' for 'a passive but discerning audience' and, in its place, has offered to democratise theatre, to make it an activity in which all engage as equals. The world behind the curtain is to be obliterated, there are not two worlds (the real world inhabited by the audience and the theatrical world masquerading as real), but one world embracing audience and performer so that the distinction between the two is broken down. The only distinction we are left with is that between those who initiate the experience and those who join in. It is an additional requirement that the experience created should not turn its back on life, but should be about life, if not part of life. These, it seems to me, are the main themes behind the modern challenge to traditional theatre.

Interpreted very simply this theory might seem to imply the prohibition of theatrical experience, such that what happens within theatre should not differ from what takes place outside it. The theory does not have this meaning, but if it did it would not challenge the 'as if' status of theatre, for it would not advocate a development within theatre but an abolition of it. What the theory is complaining about is the way in which theatrical or dramatic activities have become divorced from man's life-activities, so that dramatic activities are alienated from life-activity. The actor becomes a slave to professionalism and the audience a slave to passivity, in which case dramatic activity as something which is engaged in for its own sake ceases to exist. To insist on the theatrical being real, in this instance, means no more than that it should be a meaningful part of the lives of everyone. In none of this is theatre, as an 'as if ' phenomenon, questioned. In fact the whole theory might well be stated in terms of the way in which the 'as if ' in theatre should be presented. The notion of theatre used in this chapter is interchangeable with the notion of drama.

5

Poetry and the 'as if'

The nature of a well-known debate about poetic imagery, and it implications for the 'as if' status of poetry, is brought out in quoting from the proponents of the various standpoints involved.

Perhaps the most lucid and certainly the most famous exponent of one point of view is T. E. Hulme (often nominated as the father of imagism) who in *Speculations* says that poetry,

is not a counter-language, but a visual concrete one. It is a compromise for a language of intuition which would hand over sensations bodily. It always endeavours to arrest you, and make you continuously see a physical thing, to prevent you gliding through an abstract process. It chooses fresh epithets and fresh metaphors, not so much because they are new, and we are tired of the old, but because the old cease to convey a physical thing and become abstract counters .... Visual meaning can only be transferred by the new bowl of metaphor; prose is an old pot that lets them leak out. Images in verse are not mere decoration, but the very essence of an intuitive language.[30]

Opponents of this view define the image differently. As Fogle says in *The Imagery of Keats and Shelley*, 'Poetic imagery is to be defined broadly as analogy or comparison, having a special force and identity from the peculiarly aesthetic and concentrative richness of its contents, and the harmonious unity and fusion of its elements.[31] I. A. Richards in his attack on Hulme's thesis makes the nature of the opposition clearer.

What discourse always endeavours to do is to make us apprehend, understand, gain a realising sense of, take in, whatever it is that is being meant—which is not necessarily any physical thing. But if we say 'a realising sense', we must realise that this is not any sense necessarily, such as sense perception gives, but may be a feeling or a thought. What is essential is that we should really take in and become fully aware of whatever it is.

Words cannot, and should not attempt 'to hand over sensations bodily'; they have much more important work to do. So far from verbal language being a 'compromise for a language of intuition'—a thin but better than nothing substitute for real experience—language well used, is a completion and does what intuitions of sensations by themselves cannot do. Words are the meeting point at which regions of experience which can never combine in sensation or intuition come together. They are the occasion and the means of that growth which is the mind's endless endeavour to order itself.[32]

Fogle presses this attack against Hulme and the others. He argues that if poetry is 'a compromise for a language of intuition which would hand over sensations bodily', then it must necessarily do badly what we can all do well. Why should we concern ourselves with secondhand representations of an intuition of things which we command at first hand? Moreover, he argues, as words are not things, to what degree may they convey a physical thing? Poetry, he claims, is impoverished by this approach, and if the reader concentrates upon realising the imagery as vividly as possible, he, the reader, 'is no longer concerning himself with poetry, for poetry is words'.

As a means of assessing the issues which are involved in these claims about imagery it is necessary for them to be disentangled first.

To this end it can first of all be asked why it would be wrong to hold that there are two non-conflicting notions of poetic imagery being advanced? One of these views would be that offered by Hulme, the other offered by Fogle. If it is the case that there are two quite separate notions being offered, then we would be in a position to question the validity of the debate. There is some truth in this. Fogle's view of the poetic image puts it at the level of a figure of speech, it seems to amount to little more than a comparison, though, when at its best, a rather rich and important comparison. Whereas

Hulme is inclined, according to Fogle, to see the image as some kind of sensation brought about by reading poetry. There may be some obscurities here, but no apparent conflict. What then is the conflict about, or is it misplaced? The answer is that the conflict concerns the nature of poetry, what poetry should or should not be trying to accomplish. It is this which explains Richard's reaction to Hulme. Hulme is presented to us as the father of imagism, and this does not just mean that he believed the image, however it was to be defined, had a place in poetry. The imagists sought to reduce poetry to sequences of imagery; there were epistemological undertones to this reduction.

It was this reduction which provoked Richards's criticism. Richards tells us that words 'cannot, and should not' attempt to do what Hulme asked them to do. It is noteworthy that Richards argues in terms of 'should not' rather than 'cannot'. Whatever the merits of this debate it is quite clear that it is not essentially a contest about the nature of imagery, it is a debate about the nature of poetry, its limits and objectives. Within this context questions about the function of imagery are raised. So we might say we have two notions of poetic imagery being offered, and that what debate there is (although there is a tendency at times to debate preferred definitions) is really a debate about the purpose of poetry. However, this is not quite accurate. There is an inclination on the part of Fogle and Richards to point to some incoherence in Hulme's account of poetic imagery, thus Richards tells us that words cannot hand over sensations bodily, and Fogle asks how words in so far as they are not physical things can convey physical things. Given this additional complication it is more like the full picture to say that two distinct notions of poetic imagery are being advanced here, that one of these notions is suspected of incoherence by those who elucidate the other, and that between the two sides in this debate is another difference which is concerned with the nature of poetry. There is no reason why the debate about the nature of poetry should not be set to one side.

To what extent is Hulme's view of imagery incoherent? To begin with I do not think it is clear that Hulme thought of the poetic image as not being *in* the poem. *In* the poem, that is, as a word or as a character are said to be *in* the poem. If he did not think of it as being *in* the poem, then presumably he thought of it as being *in* the mind of the reader, and , to fit the theory, *in* the mind of the poet originally. Basically, it is this view which is thought to lead to incoherencies. There is perhaps some temptation to yield to a grotesque caricature of Hulme's theory, grotesque in so far as, if Hulme was offering a theory of this kind, it is difficult to see how he could have come to believe it. It might be claimed that Hulme first directs our attention to the poet's apprehension. At this point the poet experiences a sensation, or we might feel inclined to say, experiences imagery. The starting point then is not the world the poet experiences but the poet's experiences. The function of the poet is to produce in his audience sensations identical with his own. He does not do this by standing the audience in front of that which gives rise to his own sensations. This would be pointless, because there would be no guarantee that the sensations produced in others, by those objects, were identical with those produced in oneself by those objects; what the poet is after is that the audience should register his sensations. He achieves this by making his poem. The poem is the vehicle. It transfers or communicates the poet's sensations to the reader.

If Hulme really meant all of this, then there is little in its favour. The epistemological framework in which the theory is set makes the whole enterprise catastrophic. Here, I am referring to the notion that inevitably we are confined within a world of our own sensations. Apart from this there are other disasterous ideas. For instance, the idea that one can transfer a sensation, as one might a coin, is clearly untenable. An even greater mistake is that of supposing that the experiences which go with reading poetry constitute the having of sensations, i.e. the same sort of experiences one has when perceiving a world of objects. Here, I am excluding things like seeing the print on the page.

However, it is possible to frame an account which is close to what Hulme is saying, and which is free from these weaknesses. The poet, we might say, seeks to give his audience an impression of his way of looking at the world, to give them the feel of his own sensations. He does this by constructing a

poem which has the power to produce images in the reader.
These images are 'seeming' sensations, and this 'imaging',
which the reader embarks upon, is for him very much like the
having of those initial sensations which set the poet creating
the particular poem he offers to the reader. The poet's
business is to communicate his sense perceptions; he does this
by his poem giving rise to quasi-sense perceptions in the
reader, i.e. images. Images produced in this way
(through reading poetry) are to be known as poetic
images. According to this account it is untrue to say
poetic images are to be found *in* poetry, instead we must
say that a poetic image is that which is occasioned by
poetry.

On this account the difficulties which beset the earlier
interpretation have been eluded. There are still things wrong,
however. For instance, the limitation of the poet's expertise
to communicate his sense perceptions seems unnecessarily
severe. It is quite true that Hulme had didactic purposes and
that they lead him astray. The mistake, however, is not
philosophical. From the point of view of giving an account of
poetic imagery we get something that is much more satisfactory than is possible with the previous interpretation. Our
experience makes it obvious that poetry gives us 'imaging'
experiences, more so, generally speaking, than does prose,
though poetic prose shares this feature with genuine poetry.
This is not to say that poetic language has to be defined as
language which gives rise to such experiences, it is just that
such experiences, in the company of poetic uses of language,
are very characteristic of it. Thus, on this interpretation of
what Hulme offers us, we see him pointing to an area of
experience which is closely connected with our experience of
poetry. However, if this is what he is doing then he does little
more than indicate an area of experience. He fails to give us
anything like a full account of poetic imagery. Despite this, it
is possible to formulate something which makes up for the
gaps in Hulme's own account, and which yields a notion which
is of some use to the critic.

The first question that my interpretation of Hulme's own
account seems to invite is, 'does any "imaging" experience
which comes while reading a poem count as a poetic image, or

count as the having of a poetic image?' This question presses us into worrying about whether the effect a poem might have on one is purely subjective. This anxiety can be removed.

For the reader's image to be a poetic image it must be connected with the poem that he reads. Thus, imagery which comes as the result of one's attention turning away from the text (for instance, one is reading in the morning and has images of where one will be going in the evening) will not count. The only possible connection, in such a case, between one's reading of the poem and one's imagery is that one's boredom with the text explains, in part, one's 'imaging' experiences. In addition to there having to be a connection between the poem read and the image had, the connection needs to be of a special kind. It would not do if the connection was as loose as to allow any images, which instantiate any kind of association one might have with the text, to count as poetic images. Nor must it be so loose as to allow anyone to give a poem as many images as there are aspects of the poem which may be 'imaged'. For instance, if I read 'a red cow was grazing in the green field', it is possible for me to conjure up an image of the scene so described; I can do this deliberately, and that I do it may have nothing to do with the quality of the language that confronts me as reader. The sphere of poetic imagery would be widened if such images were allowed to count.

In order to get clear about the nature of the connection involved we need to be clear about what we are saying when we speak of imagery; although not all imagery is poetic imagery, all poetic imagery, in what I alleged to be Hulme's sense, is imagery.

If I say 'I have an image', or 'I am experiencing mental imagery,' it is appropriate to ask 'an image of what?', or 'images of what?' An image must be an image of something, it cannot just be an image. If I say 'I am experiencing an image of x' what is it that I am saying? What is meant by 'an image of'? To begin with there are different kinds of images. Thus we speak of visual, auditory, tactile, olfactory imagery. But is this of much help, because what does it mean, for instance, to say 'I am having a visual image of x'? The answer is that it means that I am seeming to see x in my mind's eye. Certainly, having a visual image of x is not seeing x. Just as certainly, having a visual image of x is not seeing an image of x. If we wished to maintain the latter view then it is hard to see how we could avoid holding the view of imagery which both Ryle[33] and Sartre[34] rightly dismiss. The only sense that can be allowed to the notion of a mental picture is that of one's seeming to see something or other in one's mind's eye. To say 'in one's mind's eye' guarantees that one only seems to see. To say one only seems to see is to say that it is like seeing but it is not, it is *as if* one sees but one does not. The experience one has in 'imaging' one has to think of as seeing, though one clearly recognises that one does not.

If on reading the poem I have an image of x (visual) then I must have seemed to see x in my mind's eye, and if this is to be a poetic image (i.e. relevantly tied to the poem and not brought about by a deliberate choice on my part) then, firstly, the x which I only seem to see must be something we can talk of as being *in* the poem (one way in which it succeeds in being in the poem is if it is described in the poem), and the image arising in consciousness must not be explained with reference to my intentions, but in terms rather of my understanding of the language used in the poem forcing me to 'image' x. Thus, with regard to the latter condition, my 'imaging' x is not voluntary except for the fact that I voluntarily undertake to read the poem, and thus allow myself to become victim of what experiences it has in store for me.

When these two conditions are observed, then we may legitimately speak of the poem as giving rise to poetic imagery. Thus, not any 'imaging' response to a poem can guarantee the poem occasions poetic imagery. The poetic image does not become, on this account, a purely subjective response. The poetic image will be an image of something which the poem makes real. Further, it will be something brought about by one's reading of the poem. That the poem brings about this response will be something adequately explained by pointing to features of the language in which the poem is written. If this point was not insisted on we should be confronted with all those cases which the psycoanalyst might provide, i.e. cases where because of some special feature of the reader's psychological constitution he 'images' something in the poem. That the poem occasions an 'imaging' response in the reader, must, if the poem gives rise to the poetic imagery, be explained by special features of the language of the poem. For instance, startling or intensely vivid uses of language would explain how the poem gives rise to 'imaging' experiences in the reader. The notion of an intensely vivid use of language is one that we may use correctly even though we have not assertained whether or not the use has in fact given rise to 'imaging' responses. Thus, a man who does not experience mental imagery will not be debarred from picking out startling uses of language. However, it will be a characteristic quality of such uses of language that they give rise to responses of a cetain kind, of which 'imaging' is but one instance. A little more will be said on this topic in the following chapter. Similarly, we can identify terrifying situations without being terrified by them, though it is characteristic of such situations that they terrify. Here, as in the case of poetic imagery, it will be what it is that one responds to, rather than something about oneself, which is the important factor in explaining one's response.

This notion of poetic image, if coherent, gives the critic a not-useless conceptual tool. There is a certain area of experience which is intimately connected with the reading of certain kinds of poetry, which the notion serves to mark off. The response involved is not purely subjective, that is to say, there can be quite legitimate debates about whether one's response is legitimate or not. Poetry, then, gives rise to 'as if' experiences, and it is not an arbitrary matter that it does. Further, to use the notion of poetic image to mark off this area of experience is not to break from tradition. It is this notion of poetic image which seems most firmly entrenched in the literature on the subject.

To accept that there is this notion is not to contest Fogle's account of the concept. The most that needs to be contested is the exclusiveness of the notion Fogle offers us. However, a criticism of Fogle's notion is its apparent uselessness. It does not appear to be a conceptual tool the critic stands badly in need of. On Fogle's account a poetic image is a comparison, or perhaps a little more fully, a comparison in a poem which organically blends with the other items of the poem. A poetic image is, then, a comparison and its function is explained in the organic theory of poetry. Here questions about what it is an image of become equivalent to what is it a comparison of. Thus, the form of the answer must be 'x with y' instead of the possibility of just 'x'. Moreover, on this view lines like,

> To what green altar, O mysterious priest,
> Lead'st thou that heifer lowing at the skies
> And all her silken flanks with garlands drest?
> (*Ode on a Grecian Urn*, J. Keats)

do not contain imagery apart from the possible metaphorical use of 'silken'. Here, then, we have a rather artificial notion of poetic imagery which amounts to little more than a comparison within the context of a poem.

No doubt Fogle is the best exponent of his own case, but it is odd that there is another notion of image which in fact we constantly use, which is closer to Fogle's own account than to Hulme's, and which does point, in a way no other term does, to a peculiar characteristic of poetry. This characteristic is displayed by other art forms, and when it is we speak of that aspect of the art form as being poetic. This notion is clearly brought out if we consider what happens in the cinema. It is not untypical in a film for a sequence of the action to close with a prolonged shot of a particular object; the point of this is that we should see a resemblance between qualities that the object possesses, and qualities possessed by the sequence of action we have witnessed. A crude example would be that where the preceding scene had seen the protagonists violently angry and the ensuing shot is of crossed logs burning fiercely. Here we would say that the blazing logs was an image of the emotions involved in the preceding scene. Comparable things happen in poetry. We speak of Donne's compass as being an image of the lovers' situation, of sleep in *Macbeth* being an image of death, of sickness and cancerous growth in *Hamlet* being an image of the political situation. In all of these cases the poet presents us with something that has qualities clearly resembling something else that he is presenting us with. Where this happens there is surely a strong inclination to speak of the organic structure of the work. It is not that the poet gives us a comparison, but that he provides us with something which we proceed to compare with something else he gives us. The reasons why poets should do this are too multifarious to specify.

This account is one we must give of poetic imagery, and it seems close enough to Fogle's to prompt speculation as to whether it is not this account that Fogle thinks he is giving. It must be admitted, however, that Fogle's subsequent treatment of imagery in the rest of his book suggests that he *works* with a notion which is not far removed from Hulme's. It must be emphasised that the account of poetic imagery just given does not clash with the earlier account. Both accounts point to features which are very typical of our experience of poetry.

I conclude, therefore, that poetry gives rise characteristically to 'as if ' experiences, and objects in so far as it contains (a) evocative language which induces 'imaging' responses, and (b) items which have to be thought of as if they were other items, although this latter case is ambiguous between my notion of the 'as if' and Vaihinger's: the resolution of the ambiguity depends upon the extent to which the resemblance is that of verisimilitude.

6

Literature in general and the 'as if'

In this chapter I shall turn to a more general consideration of the 'as if' in literature. I shall try to illuminate the activity of *making it real* through an analysis of those techniques which an author employs to make it real (e.g. the technique of evocation). No doubt a more exhaustive analysis of the techniques involved in this activity would be worthwhile, but in this context it is enough to indicate the general 'as if' character of the various art forms, rather than give a detailed analysis of the many ways in which the sphere of the 'as if' is produced.

When considering the role of imagination in art, in earlier chapters, it was suggested that the novelist's task was one of trying to make whatever he was writing about real for himself in writing about it. In addition, it was suggested that if he succeeded in this he would have reason to think he had made whatever he had written about real for the reader, as he (the reader) reads.

Firstly, I shall try to clarify this suggestion that it is the author's task to try to make it real. Secondly, I shall point to the complexity of 'making it real', and lastly, I shall investigate the status of judgments concerning evocation.

It should be noted that books which are correctly described by the following descriptions are not necessarily novels:

(a) A book which contains more than fifty-thousand words, tells a story, though the story is pure fabrication.

(b) A book which contains more than fifty-thousand words and which tells a story of a person's life.

It should be noted also that books which are thus correctly described are not necessarily not novels.

A business report to shareholders can be a massive document; it can tell a story, the story of the company's finances over the last year; the items it lists can be pure fabrication, it being the director's intention to dupe the shareholders. A business report displaying these features would not thereby be a novel. Biographies are long books, and by definition tell the story of a person's life, but not all biographies are novels although some are. For example, Irving Stone's *Lust for Life* is clearly a novel, whereas Taylor's *Bismark* is clearly not.[35] No doubt a book which is long enough, which contains characters and whose content is purely fictional, where the fictional items are in the main interconnected in a sufficiently varied and complex manner, will be a novel. Here, my earlier remarks about the construction of fiction show what kind of a link exists between such constructions and the activity of making it real. Earlier I distinguished between the construction of fiction and the telling of lies by saying that the former activity was one of only appearing or seeming to make empirical claims, whereas the latter was one of making empirical claims that normally, at most, appeared to be true. However, a fictional content is not a necessity for the novel. Many autobiographies we classify as novels and many biographies as well. To discover, having read a book, that everything it speaks of actually happened is not to have doubts about it being a novel, though it is to upset the judgment that it is fiction. War stories, *Lust for Life*, etc., are deemed novels in the light of stylistic considerations. We can write about things in different ways, and it is the special way in which we write that brings our writing into the area of the novel. The special way of writing has everything to do with the making of what one is writing about real. The following analogy breaks down as an analogy at certain points, but it usefully indicates what I mean.

There is, I think, a difference between the way the working class report on past meetings with other persons, and the way middle class persons do this. For example, it is not just the bad grammar which makes the following improbable as a conversation between dons.

'Dot said to I, "I'm not 'aving it, I'm not putting up with it anymore, I've worked for 'im when 'e was ill, I've gone without meself to put clothes on 'is back." So I said "Go on, kick 'im out poor old devil, if you can. See 'ow you feel then."

"It's alright for you," she said, "you don't 'ave to put up with 'im stinking out the place all the time." '

I suspect a middle-class rendering of a comparable predicament might be.

'Dorothy impressed on me the sacrifices she had made for father, and it struck me she is no longer prepared to look after him. I stressed she was too warm-hearted to give him up now, after all these years, but of course she was in a position to point out that I did not have the burden of looking after him.'

The middle-class rendering obscures the original situation. We learn a number of facts about it, but we are not brought face to face with it. It is important that we learn of Dorothy's views, but not important that we learn of Dorothy at a particular moment in a particular situation. That Dorothy was standing in her kitchen, in pink slippers, showing by the way she speaks her words and by the faces she makes how she feels, is unimportant. The concrete situation is forsaken for generalisations. In contrast, Dot is brought to life. We get her very words and we get them plus intonation. We can even get, and often do, the words spoken with the appropriate facial gestures and body movements. The one who tells us of Dot, becomes Dot. We regard her as such.

There is a stylistic difference here, and its effects go beyond style. In the first example we get quotes, but not in the second. This difference affects the focus. It affects what it is possible to get out of the two accounts.

It would be quite wrong to insist that the particular stylistic feature exhibited in the first account be present in the novel, and those exhibited by the second example be absent. For one thing the second example might constitute a fictional item within the context of a larger fiction. There is no stylistic feature that must apply if the author succeeds in making his subject real for the reader, there is no one stylistic feature which if employed guarantees this success. Despite this the kind of difference which exists between these examples is like the difference between the work of non-fiction that we do regard as a novel, and the work of non-fiction that we do not. The difference in generalised form is one of making it real. The first example makes the past conversation real in a way that the second example tries, almost explicitly, not to do.

The kind of prose which gives life to the subject it relates, is the kind of prose which is central to our notion of a novel. Our involvement in a novel is something mediated by it seeming as though we have been confronted with the persons and events narrated. It is the quality of the events being brought to life on the page, of the characters moving through their environments, that is so characteristic of one's experience of the novel.

These remarks about the novel should not be construed as implying either (a) that the novelist is condemned to write of the particularities of the world and men's actions; (there are novels where the characters stand still, but where inner turbulence betrays the facade—here one can either report the facts or bring the reader to grips with the inner goings-on) or (b) that the mathematician, who in his textbook brings his subject to life, does exactly what I say the novelist does. (The force of the notion 'bring to life' in this case is not at all what it is in the context of the novel. The mathematician who brings his subject to life does not do much more than make his subject interesting to those who otherwise might not find it so. The novelist who brings the events to life on the page makes it for the reader as though he (the reader) is experiencing or witnessing those events, when he is not.)

The historian, who provides us with a number of facts about social conditions in England in the eighteenth century, may leave us with a clearer picture, even a vivid picture, of social conditions at that time, but there remains a very real difference between being made to come as though face to face with those conditions, and forming a picture for oneself of those conditions on the strength of some newly provided facts. None of this is to say that a history book is barred *a priori* from being a novel, nor from being as 'as if' object.

If standardly, or typically, the novelist must make it all real, there is at least one thing this should not be interpreted as meaning. It must not be interpreted as meaning that he must write in accordance with the critical doctrine of *realism*. The incidents in a novel can read very real, be very convincing, without there being incidents beyond the novel with which those in the novel correspond. Similar points hold in other areas and thus bring out the force of this point. For example, there are some situations on the stage, which if taken as intended representations of reality would have to be construed as grotesque misrepresentations, and yet, despite this, it can really seem to be the case that these situations are taking place on the stage; they can be done convincingly. Further, that descriptions taking the form 'x looks like y' are intrinsic to our description of pictures qua pictures (where x stands for the materials used) does not mean that there must be some y which x looks like. In fact, x can look very much like y without thereby conjuring into existence y. There is a difference between making the events and the characters of a novel real, and them being realistic.[36] By analogy, what the conjuror is supposed to have done, which we all know he has not done, may be highly improbable, but he can give a convincing impression that he has done it nevertheless; in fact if he is a good conjuror, he must. Similarly, whether or not the contents of a novel are realistic, i.e. correspond, more or less, with our experience of the world, is unimportant, whereas, whether or not they are made real for us is crucial. A further point is that a conjuror faced with an audience of fellow magicians will not be allowed to get away with naive tricks that deceive less sophisticated audiences. In fact, things which are extremely unconvincing can satisfy some people as being very convincing. The difference between the good novel and the bad is much more like the difference between a trick well done and a trick fumbled, than fashionable doctrines would allow. This view would be wrong if the ways of making it all real solely concerned the ways of rendering a content, for certainly in distinguishing between good and bad novels we are vitally concerned with what the novel is about, certainly as much concerned with it as we are with the way in which the novel renders what it is about. But in conjuring it is as much the complexity and internal coherence of what appears to have been done which makes the illusion convincing, as it is the way in which the appearances are simulated. In other words, the complexity and detail of your creations may be one way of making them more real for the reader than they otherwise would be.

Making it real is an activity central to the activity of producing a novel. It involves giving the reader quasi-experience of, and producing in him quasi-involvement with, the world of the novel. It does not amount to a doctrine of realism, although in its own right it has critical repercussions.

My second task concerns a brief analysis of some of the activities and notions which are bound up with the notion 'making it real'.

Consider the following list: to provoke, to stimulate, to move, to evoke, to suggest, to convey, to portray. These notions have their similarities and their differences. To provoke, to stimulate, to move, must be distinguished from the other notions on the list. To provoke, or to stimulate, or to move, are activities different in kind from evoking, suggesting, portraying. If I provoke you, or stimulate you, or move you, I do something to you; the activity of evoking you is very much more like the activity of painting your picture. I can provoke anger in you, but not evoke it in you, though my words may evoke x's anger for you. If I provoke anger in you, you are provoked, but if I evoke the mood for you, you are not thereby evoked. Though I can be said to have evoked the mood, suggested the tension, portrayed the scene, without necessarily having affected anyone, nevertheless 'evoking', 'suggesting' and 'portraying' all normally have their effects. The writer does not wait for an audience to evoke or portray, etc., these are things which he does in writing, whereas he cannot know that he has provoked or stimulated, or moved anyone until the work has been received. In the former case a writer *may not* judge he has evoked the mood until the critics have had a chance to assess it, but logically he *cannot* judge that he has provoked someone until the reaction to his work has been registered. This kind of difference is not so clearly recorded if we turn to the adjectives 'provocative', 'stimulating', 'moving', 'evocative', 'suggestive'. A work could be all of these things though no one found it so. Of course, that a work is evocative entails that it evokes something, whereas if provocative it is not entailed that it provokes something, but if evocative it is not entailed that it evokes something for someone.

That a work is some, or all, of these things may be important in making its subject real, and that an author embarks on some, or all, of these activities may be important in achieving the same goal. As far as these lists suggest, the process of making it real for the reader contains at least two distinct elements. Thus, one may increase the chances of the reader finding it all real by engaging him, by involving him, by stimulating him, by moving him. In other words, one brings the reader face to face with the events through saddening him by the events, but one also does it by portraying the events vividly, and evoking their atmosphere; often the two processes interact or reinforce each other.

'Making real' is not always a matter of evoking. To write evocatively at certain points in the novel would be to produce a discordant note. For example, in places it may be necessary to write the flattest, most unevocative prose in order to heighten the drama, and intensify the reader's involvement. That this is so points to the criteria of evocation, by this I mean the criteria of judgments with the form 'it (the work) evokes y', as opposed to judgments with the form 'it (the work) evokes y for me'. This difference is like the difference between 'it seems to be the case that p' and 'it seems to me to be the case that p'. That x evokes y does not follow from the fact that it evokes it for me, anymore than it follows from it seems to me that p, that it seems that p. The criteria of evocation, in the case of writing, depends upon the kind of prose which is employed. The following seems reasonably clear: prose which is dull, flat, prosaic, pedestrian, formal, official, plain, is unevocative, whereas that which is colourful, rich, poetic, decorative, vivid, etc., is evocative. Seeing that prose of the latter category is evocative, will be closely connected with seeing it as prose of that category, (more closely connected for example, than is the poetic image I have and the startling use of language I read). One would be able to see that it was a startling use of language though it gave rise to no 'imaging' experiences in one. This will not be the case with seeing that the piece is evocative and seeing that the style of the language is of the second category. The relationship between evocation and poetic imagery is such that the piece which provokes the image certainly evokes what the image is an image of. The piece will do all of this if the language in which it is written is particularly startling or vivid. Less vivid uses of language, yet uses belonging to the second category specified, will be evocative though not giving rise to imagery. The poetic image is formed with the most vivid uses of language. However, the suggestion is not that those passages which are the most real are those provoking the most imagery. It seems fairly clear that the way to make a long sequence of events real for the reader has little to do with presenting him with the intensity of language required by a sonnet; in this context such intensity would just get in the way of gaining a realising sense of the sequence of events.

Most of my comments have been about the novel, but I think they apply to many kinds of poetry, certainly to all lyrical poetry, as well as to the short story and to the literary aspects of drama.

7

The status of propositions within fictions

n the last three chapters what has taken place has been an nvestigation of the connections between the 'as if ' sphere and terature. It has emerged that in literature (and this is espe- ially so of fiction) a primary aim must be to make it all real. But how are we to regard the language of fiction? For nstance, do all novels contain propositions, and if we sup- osed they did not, would this not make for difficulties in our aining a sense of reality from the novel? Alternatively, do ome novels contain propositions all of which are false, and vould this give rise to comparable difficulties in attaining a ense of reality from such novels? Or, are there some novels vhich do not contain propositions, but nevertheless must be reated as though they do, in order for us to gain this sense of eality from them? In my opinion none of these implied haracterisations of the language of fiction need be accepted. There are good reasons for holding that the language of iction contains statements which may be both true and false i.e. statements which are not precluded from being true in so ar as they occur in a fictional context). If this is so, then we vill have something quite sufficient for showing that deriving sense of reality from works of fiction is unproblematic. However, the view of the language of fiction just offered is ontroversial.

Miss Macdonald maintained that fictional language is either true nor false.[37] Thus, in saying 'Emma Woodhouse as lived nearly twenty-one years in the world' Jane Austen ould not be saying something true or false, which is also to ay no investigation could yield evidence for its truth or alsity. This contention lends support to another contention, amely, what is not in a piece of fiction is absent for all time; hus, the number of Lady Macbeth's children in the play *Macbeth* is indeterminate, and the subsequent history of olita no task for an historian. Of course, investigations of the vorld lead to views of the world, and views of the world affect

our interpretations of novels and plays, and as Miss Mac
Donald claims elsewhere, novels and plays are the sum of ou
interpretations. However, in one sense of 'what is a piece o
fiction', we do not interpret what is in it, and further a
interpretation has to be an interpretation of something. W
do not interpret that Mr Darcy was rich, that Hamlet sen
Rosencrantz and Guildenstern to their death, that the Wife o
Bath enjoyed money and sex, anymore than we interpret tha
there are holes in the wall that need plastering; these ar
strictly cases of finding out. An investigation of the world i
not a way of finding out the content of fictional forms, nor i
way of assessing the truth or falsity of those proposition
which say what this content is.

Before proceeding there are two objections to the thesis
am supporting that must be met. To be clear the thesis I an
supporting is but part of Miss Macdonald's thesis, which is t
say I wish to disassociate myself, for reasons I shall give later
from her contention that fictional language is neither true no
false, though I wish to associate myself with her contentio
that no investigation of the world could yield evidence for th
truth or falsity of such uses of language. One objection to th
thesis I support would be that within a fictional context a
author might well report on places he had visited, on incident
he had witnessed, etc. My reply is that there must be
difference between fiction and biography, and fiction an
newspaper reports, such that there is a sensible differenc
between fictional biography and biography, and fictiona
reports and reports. An essential feature of fiction, as wit
lying, is that it is made up. It is only when this fact has bee
admitted that the second objection asserts itself. The objec
tion states that though fiction is made up, there is no logica
restriction on its being coincidentally true of the world, thus
man suffering from amnesia may wrongly believe he killed hi
wife, and subsequently, on examination, make up a story so a
not to incriminate himself, and this story might be found b
the police to coincide with the facts, and similarly it may b
argued with fictional incidents and 'statements'.

To deal with this objection I will consider an analogou
problem which is met in an examination of statements i
general. The statement made in nineteenth-century Englan

hat 'in England children under 14 years work in the mines', is
rue, whereas the same construction of words used in twen-
ieth-century England would be false, if asserted as a statement about how things are today. The point about this
example is that the statement made in nineteenth-century
England, if true, is always true, for in considering what
statement this statement is, i.e. what the linguistic construction asserts, we must be interested in what was meant by what
was said, and in what the words were used to refer to. The
reason why the statement 'in England children under 14 work
in the mines' can be false in the twentieth-century is dependent upon what the words are used to talk about, i.e. what is
said by them. Such considerations point to different assertions
being made with the same words, and different assertions
having to differ in more respects than their truth or falsity,
otherwise they cannot differ in truth or falsity. What is
involved in this supervenient account of truth must equally
apply to using language to construct fictions. Thus, it is either
the case that the statement in Huxley's novel, 'But she had
been well brought up in the habits of the strictest control' is
true if the statement made of a real Marjory Carling, who
knew a real Walter Bidlake, which had the same liguistic
form, is true, or it is the case that the statement in Huxley's
novel is not the same statement as made of a real Marjory
Carling. The issue is resolved in this case by ascertaining what
the words are used to refer to, and it is obvious that Huxley
does not use them to refer to a real Marjory Carling, for if he
did the objection itself would fail, based as it is on coincidental
truth, and the notion that that which is essentially fictional is
made up. To admit that what authors say is made up is already
to indicate that their statements are different from those
statements made by those who do not make up what they say.
What Huxley *qua* fiction writer was writing about was a
fictional Marjory Carling, and because the words he uses to
write about her may well be the words used to write about a
real Marjory Carling, it can in no way follow that he was also
writing about a real Marjory Carling. In objecting to the view
that one cannot test the truth or falsity of fictional language by
investigating the world, one cannot argue by analogy from the
coincidental truth of an assertion which is supposed to be a lie,

to the coincidental truth of a fictional statement in fiction. It is
perhaps true that the assertion 'x is brown', which is supposed
to be a lie, may not be false, and that the way of deciding this
will involve an investigation of the world, but the reason for
this is that a lie, unlike a statement in fiction, is a statement
about the world, though thought by the liar to be a false
statement about the world. A statement in fiction may *appear*
to be a statement about the world, but it is certainly not a
statement about the world, and so not a statement about the
world which is thought to be false. It may be noted here how
useful is Miss Macdonald's distinction between deception and
conviction with reference to the distinction between lies and
fiction, and it may also be noted how useful is the inclusion of
the word *appears*, or one might substitue 'seems', for there is
no *a priori* barrier to prevent something which seems or
appears to be saying something about the world to seem or
appear to be true; thus we have a correct account of the
situation in which people really believe the Archers exist.

I want now to give a more detailed analysis of why the
objection based on the notion of coincidental truth does not
hold with regard to fictional language, and here I must depart
from Miss Macdonald's views, for I shall argue that 'true' and
'false' are correct terms for characterising fictional language
(which she does not), but that the criteria for assessing
whether a statement in fiction is true or false are not the
criteria suggested by looking around the world for coincidences. To show a statement in fiction is true or false on other
grounds than those of looking for coincidences, and on
grounds which are inapplicable to deciding the truth or falsity
of that statement with which it is held to be coincidentally
true, is to show that it is not that statement with which it shares
a common linguistic form and which is true of the world.

To remain clear I set out the following:

Key
MC stands for Marjory Carling
x stands for any predicate
N stands for novel
FMC stands for fictional Marjory Carling
B stands for biography

BMC stands for biographical Marjorie Carling
RMC stands for real Marjorie Carling

Statement		*Notes about its context*
(a)	'MC is x'	(1)	of FMC in N
(b)	MC is x	(2)	of FMC but not in N
(c)	'MC is x'	(3)	in B, and of RMC
(d)	MC is x	(4)	of RMC, not in B, but the grounds for its assertion being the fact of (c) (3) or an equivalent in B
(e)	MC is x	(5)	of RMC, but not necessarily the background of (d) (4)

In the light of this schema the following propositions are to be assessed as true or false:

1 If (a) (1) is true then (b) (2) is true.
2 If (b) (2) is true then (a) (1) is true.
3 If (c) (3) is true then (d) (4) and (e) (5) are true.
4 If (d) (4) is true then (c) (3) and (e) (5) are true.
5 If (e) (5) is true then (c) (3) and (d) (4) are true.
6 If (a) (1) is true then (e) (5) is true.
7 If (e) (5) is true then (a) (1) is true.

From her article it would appear that Miss Macdonald would have denied the truth of 1 and 2, admitted the truth of 3, 4 and 5, and denied the truth of 6 and 7. I shall argue in contrast that 1 and 2 are true, or are true with one rather irrelevant reservation.

To begin with, it should be apparent that (b) (2) could well be true or false. We have institutions like examinations where one's knowledge of fiction is tested, and the characteristic answer to an examination question is (b) (2). Thus we might be asked 'Was Mr Pickwick bald?', or 'Did Arabella trap Jude into marriage?', and of course it is true that Mr Pickwick was bald, and that Arabella trapped Jude into marriage. Another point to note is that (b) (2) need not be true or false, for what can be asserted in (b) (2) might be genuinely indeterminate, as in 'Lady Macbeth in the play *Macbeth* had four children'. If (b) (2) can be true or false, it is difficult to know what

objections there could be to construing (a) (1) in the same
way. Perhaps the only objection would be that of asking for
the grounds of its truth or falsity. However, statements
which occur in fiction are often only to be correctly understood by considering their truth or falsity. Often in novels the
characters speak, and rarely in the theatre or the cinema does
the author speak. It is open to characters to lie, to say that
which is false, and it would be a peculiar view of fiction which
asserted that characters always told the truth, said only that
which was true, or never said anything true of false. Nor does
this just apply to characters, for authors might tell lies, or,
more simply, say that which is untrue. A naive example of
authors saying, via the fictional context, something false is
evidenced by the institution of proof reading. One may well
contradict oneself in one's novel, after all a novel is a long
book. At one point in the novel the author might write that
the wedding took place on the 5th of August, whereas everything else in the novel makes it clear that it was the 6th of
August on which the wedding took place, in the light of other
evidence, evidence in the novel, it is obvious that it is false that
the wedding took place on the 5th of August. It is undeniable
that if we are to have a novel at all, then not everything in that
novel can be false, for there are no grounds other than
those provided by the novel for ascertaining whether that
which is in the novel is false or not. However, this is to say not
everything in the novel can be false, and not to say that
particular statements in the novel can be neither true nor
false. Of course (a) (1) may be but a passing comment, and
there may be no reference to it anywhere else in the novel, but
then that there is no other reference to what is asserted by (a)
(1), far from it pointing to (a) (1) being neither true nor false,
points to (a) (1) being true, just as certainly as it points to (b)
(2) being true. Another objection might be that the only
grounds for (b) (2) being true is (a) (1), but not (a) (1) being
true; however, this is to make a mistake, for the grounds
which make (b) (2) true are those where there is no evidence
in the novel to suggest (a) (1) might be false, and of course if
subsequent fictional events showed (a) (1) to be false, then (b)
(2) would be false also. Thus, I conclude that 1 and 2 are true
and are true because they are both about FMC, the truth

about FMC being found in the novel. The reason for (a) (1) being true when it is intended as a lie is not just that (b) (2) is true but that (a) (1) and (b) (2) are about FMC, and (b) (2) is true of FMC, thus (a) (1) is true of FMC also. There is a possible exception to my views here because of the possibility of a FN occuring in N. In FN in N there may be a FMC, and what is true of FMC will depend upon which FMC one is talking about, the one in N or FN. Such possibilities should give cause for reservations about the truth of 1 and 2, but the reservations are hardly important.

3, 4 and 5 are all true. They all amount to the same statement, for their three constituents are references to different utterances of the same statement. The fact that the grounds for these different utterances will not be, or may not be, the same is clearly unimportant.

6 and 7 are false, and perhaps 6 more obviously than 7. If we read in the novel 'MC is x' it can in no way follow, even if true, that (e) (5) is true, because the author's remarks are not about RMC but FMC. As with the example of children working in the mines, it is what one is talking about which determines whether a statement is the same statement as another, and that the novelist is not talking about RMC is admitted within the front cover of his novel. Of 7 we may say, it may be true that RMC is rich, and this may be said of FMC in N, but FMC might not be rich; that it has been asserted in the novel that she is rich might be the result of the author employing irony, or of character y being mistaken about her, even if she was rich the grounds for (a) (1) being true would not be the truth of a linguistically identical assertion about RMC. This would, of course, be a case of a genuine coincidence, in the sense that an identical linguistic construction was used to make different assertions both of which were true; but that is all that can be said.

A further objection to my thesis might be the following. Suppose in a detective story we read the detective's question 'What can one see in Paris?' and the suspect's reply 'Nelson's Column', would it not be the case that by investigating the real world one would determine whether this claim, in the work of fiction, was true or not, and would it not be the author's intention that we should employ such knowledge in order to conclude that the man who says 'Nelson's Column', is the suspect? The reply to this is that whether or not Nelson's Column is not in Paris in the novel is entirely up to the author, which is to contend that the fictional world can differ from the real world in more fantastic ways than the possibility latent in this example suggests. We do not investigate the real world in order to ascertain that Nelson's Column, in the novel, is not in Paris, but rather investigate the rules of the novel. The conviction that the geography of the fictional world does not differ from the geography of the real world may help to set up anticipations not unconnected with one's enjoyment of a work, but nonetheless it will not be some fact about the real world which will make the statements of the novel true.

A more fundamental objection than anything so far offered might proceed as follows. The account which has been given is too superficial. The problem about whether fiction contains statements, or if it does whether they can be true, only really asserts itself when we come to offer a theory about truth. The answers to these questions cannot be adequate, therefore, unless an accommodating theory of truth has been provided, and it is clear that such a theory is absent in the account given so far. If we grant that statements occur in fiction, must we not say of the statement 'Mr Pickwick is bald' that in so far as it is false that there is a Mr Pickwick, it must be false that Mr Pickwick is bald. If one wants to say, despite this, that the statement is true, for the sort of reasons that have been given, is one really saying anymore than the proposition 'Dickens said "Mr Pickwick is bald" ' is true? If this is all that is meant then one might as well say so, for it avoids the contradiction in holding that it is true and false that Mr Pickwick is bald, and more importantly it steers us clearly away from three-valued logic (for instance, ' "Lady Macbeth in the play *Macbeth* had four children" is indeterminate', becomes equivalent to ' "Shakespeare neither implies nor does not imply that Lady Macbeth had four children" is true'), and also steers us away from dangerous notions of two kinds of worlds and two kinds of facts; i.e. it steers us away from propositions which might cause us to reject very adequate theories about truth.

The forceful aspect of this argument is that the statements in fiction are false because they lack proper referents whereas there are a number of truths we may state about these statements concerning the relationship between them and their author. It is the truth about this relationship which is really all that is referred to in the account this objection seeks to expose.

This objection begins to come unstuck when we grasp the complexity of relations between author and the statements he writes. The relations are complex enough to make us pause and contemplate, in certain cases, which relation holds, and this hesitancy can set in long after we have made up our mind about the truth or falsity of the statement we locate in the work. For instance, suppose we encounter the line in a Shakespeare play spoken by x which is 'He was drinking all this night; I can vouch for it.' Suppose, according to the account I have provided, we want to say the two statements involved are false, how would we render this in terms of the objection? Here, if it is certainly Shakespeare's play we can say 'Shakespeare wrote "He was drinking all this night; I can vouch for it" ' is true. But this cannot be equivalent to what, on the account given, would be a pronouncement of the falsity of the two statements, for we could relate Shakespeare in the same way to any other statement in his play, i.e. to statements which, on the account given, we would want to say were true. The same, and other, difficulties would beset 'Shakespeare thought . . .', 'Shakespeare asserted . . .' or 'Shakespeare said . . .'. A more likely contender might appear to be 'Shakespeare implied that "He was drinking all this night; I can vouch for it" is false' is true. But why is it a proposition about what Shakespeare *implied* that we are pronouncing true? If asked whether the play implied the two statements were false, we might feel inclined to reply it was rather that the play made it clear that they were, i.e. it was something more obvious than implication. Of course, this need not be worrying, for it can be said that if this is so a more likely contender would be 'Shakespeare makes it clear that "He was drinking all this night; I can vouch for it" is false' is true. But suppose Shakespeare makes it clear within the front cover of his play that the work is pure fiction. Will it not be the case that it will be true of each and every statement in the play that Shakespeare has made it clear that they are false? How, then, are we to express the difference which the account given claims to adequately express by saying that some statements in fiction are true and others false? Possibly we might fidget around and come up with some statements that more adequately express Shakespeare's relationship with these statements in his play at the same time as reflecting the true/false distinction in the account under attack, but whether or not there is such a refinement is a needless query. What is clear is that which of the possible relations between author and the statements in his works of fiction holds and, at the same time, reflects the true/false distinction is a complicated business. In accordance with the account given we would be able to decide that the two propositions in Shakespeare's play were false long before deciding about the true/false-reflecting-relation which holds between Shakespeare and these two statements. If this is so it seems clear that in saying 'MC is x' is true, one is not really saying, only in a misleading way, something about the relationship between Huxley and the proposition.

The accusation that no theory of truth has been provided, must be conceded, but then, why is a theory of truth required? Why is it not enough to point out that 'true' and 'false' are words we would use naturally in this context, and that it is possible to specify conditions for their correct use. We do not regard statements in fiction as being necessarily false, because we do not regard them as making assertions about the world. If this is so, it is not clear that there are philosophical problems which cast doubts on our being able to obtain a sense of reality from a work of fiction.

8

The 'as if' in visual art

In *Art and Illusion*[38] Gombrich's target is not the whole sphere
of the plastic arts; in this book his problems surround the
history of what is called 'representational' painting. From
what has gone before it might seem clear that what is called
'representational' painting must be thought of in 'as if' terms.
It would be difficult then not to link my treatment of 'representational' visual art with Gombrich's in some way. Gombrich does, of course, hold views about other aspects of visual
art and I, also, must give some account of these other aspects.

For my purposes a useful starting point is R. Wollheim's
inaugural lecture *On Drawing an Object*.[39] From section 22 of
this lecture it becomes both relevant and fruitful. It is relevant
because it provides a good starting point to the problems
Gombrich gives rise to, it is fruitful, in my opinion, because of
the way in which Wollheim tries to loosen our notion of
'representation';[40] I shall use certain aspects of his treatment
of 'representation' to apply to those spheres of painting
generally thought of as 'non-representational'.

To begin with, however, there are other issues which need
to be opened. They concern what it is that Gombrich is saying
and how Wollheim interprets this thesis. In *On Drawing an
Object* Wollheim sets out two contrasting views on representation. One of these is attributed to Gombrich, the other to no
one in particular. It seems that Wollheim thinks of the second
view as being quite common. However, it seems to me that
the view attributed to Gombrich is not Gombrich's view, or if
his view not his main view, and that the other view, which is
regarded by Wollheim as the diametric opposite of what is
alleged to be Gomrich's view, is not so clearly not Gombrich's
view. Perhaps quotations from Wollheim's Lecture will help
to bring out the views which he holds to be mistaken, one of
which he attributes to Gombrich.

But now I must pause and consider this new phrase, which has
apparently been so useful, and ask, What is it to see something as a

93

representation? A question that I rather dread, because I have so little constructive to say in answer to it. I shall begin with a view that has of recent years been canvassed with great brilliance but which I am convinced is fundamentally wrong, and that is that to see something as a representation of a lion or a bowl of fruit is to be disposed to some degree or other, though probably never totally, to take it for a lion or a bowl of fruit: the degree to which we are so disposed being an index of its versimilitude or goodness as a representation. That representation is a kind of partial or inhibited illusion, working for one sense or from one point of view and that to see something as a representation is to enter into this illusion so far as is practicable, is a view that has obvious attractions: even if only because it offers to explain a very puzzling phenomenon in terms of one that is easy and accessible.[41]

The rejection of the idea that representation is a kind of partial or inhibited illusion might will lead us to the view, which can be regarded as its diametric opposite, that representation is a kind of code or convention. On this view, to see a drawing as a representation of something is no longer to take it, or to be disposed to take it, for that thing: it is rather to understand that thing by it. Now this view not merely avoids the grossness of assimilating all works of representation to *trompe-l'oeil*, it has the added advantage that it can allow for the way in which we are able simultaneously to take in, or admire, a drawing as a configuration and as a representation. For when we turn to other cases which are indubitably those of a code or convention, there seems to be no difficulty over any analogous bifurcation of interest. Can we not attend at once to the typography of a book and to what the book says? Do we have to deflect our attention from the beauty of the script to appreciate the melancholy of the poetry it conveys?

We get in Gombrich a number of arguments which link art with illusion. It is not clear in what way this connection is made. It is not obvious that it is made as Wollheim suggests. Secondly, it is in Gombrich that we encounter the notion of explaining representation via a cryptogram. But more than this. It is Gombrich who uses the notion of 'schemata'. It is Gombrich who draws our attention to the conventions involved in constructing and understanding schemata. It is Gombrich who speaks of what is involved in reading the image. Reading the image is a matter of learning to interpret the schema used in the construction of it. In the circumstances most readers of Gombrich could be forgiven for viewing him as having offered the explanation of representational painting in terms of it being some kind of language, some kind of code, which we must learn to read or unravel. Wollheim claims that this view is the diametric opposite of the view that representation has to be accounted for as some kind of partial or inhibited illusion. Gombrich is credited with the first view, it is hard to see how he can avoid holding the second. If he holds both it is difficult to see how he can avoid being committed to some contradiction. To avoid a contradiction it would be necessary to explain how that which is to be read can give rise to an illusion of that which it is a code about through its being read. In my judgment, I see no way in which, in *Art and Illusion,* Gombrich explains away any such contradiction in this fashion. If the contradiction could be avoided it would be of little importance when it is the case that both views, though reconciled, yield inadequate accounts for representation. That they are inadequate is something quickly made clear in *On Drawing an Object.*

The main objection to the illusionistic theory made by Wollheim is that our experience in front of the *trompe-l'oeil* is markedly unlike our normal experience of representational painting. Really this is to say that our normal experience of the representational in art is unlike our experience of illusions. In contrast to Gombrich, it may be successfully maintained that one may attend simultaneously to both the picture and its texture, and that this is inconsistent with one's response to a picture involving a confrontation with an illusory x, where the picture is a picture of x. Gombrich holds that to see the picture and to see the texture involves a switch, and Wollheim takes the reason for this to be Gombrich's view that seeing a picture of x involves confrontation with an illusory x.

The main objection given by Wollheim to the conventionalist account is that all sorts of things would, in terms of the theory, count as representations that normally would not be regarded as such. Thus Wollheim suggests that to cut a picture into pieces and to rearrange the pieces in accordance with

principles, such that in applying the principles to the rearrangement one could derive from it all the information that it
was possible to derive previously from the unmolested picture, would be, according to the theory being attacked, to
have produced a representation. Wollheim thinks it obvious
that this is not so.

These attacks on these theories are in themselves quite
adequate. However, are these theories correctly attributed to
Gombrich? With reference to the second theory I think it
must be so. The first view, however, I think is more difficult to
attribute to Gombrich. Gombrich himself indicates differences between *trompe-l'oeil* and the normal run of representational paintings. Certainly, Gombrich claims to be interested in illusion in art, after all his book is called *Art and
Illusion*, but this does not mean that he is concerned to
advance the view that the picture of x confronts us with an
illusory x. Consider Gombrich's comments on Kenneth
Clarke 'stalking and illusion'. Is it so clear that here the
illusion stalked is the picture of x yielding a situation which
may deceive us into thinking that x confronts us? Clarke's
difficulty seems to involve the switch from paint to picture,
and not that of from paint to the illusion of actual confrontation with the subject of the picture. His difficulty is akin to
switching from reading the duck/rabbit as a duck and then as
a rabbit. A deceptive element here concerns what Gombrich
is prepared to classify as illusion. It needs to be noted that for
Gombrich illusions include the Frazer Spiral, the Spreading
Effect, the duck/rabbit, mirror images and representational
paintings. It is clear that Gombrich's use of the word 'illusion'
is eccentric. I suspect the uncontaminated view would be that
no illusion was involved in the switch from seeing the paint to
seeing the picture. This uncontaminated view can lead one
away from the interpretation of Gombrich where the switch is
seen as indicating illusion. Woolheim argues that we can
attend both to picture and texture simultaneously, and in this
he intends to deny that we have an illusion of what the picture
is a picture of. It is because he thinks that Gombrich is
concerned with this illusion that Woolheim sees him as being
concerned to deny the possibility of these simultaneous perceptions. If he was concerned with this illusion it would seem

he must deny the simultaneity of these perceptions. However, I am suggesting that Woolheim's claim that no switch is involved can be construed as a denial that an illusion must occur because of the necessity of the switch. It is an illusion in virtue of the switches which do occur that, I suggest, Gombrich is concerned to assert. In other words, he tries to account for the fact of seeing what is in front of you as a painting, by claiming that what is involved is transcending the physical particular by means of an illusion. The paint becomes picture by means of an illusion. But the illusion is not that which, if we knew no better, would lead us to suppose that it was not a picture that we saw but what it was a picture of, rather the illusion seems to be that of there being a picture. It is the picture which for Gombrich is the illusion. In a sense the theme of *Art and Illusion* is how material is transformed to yield a picture. For Gombrich it would seem this theme is that of how an illusion is produced. It is this claim about the intrusion of illusion into the representational aspect of painting which, in Gombrich, needs to be reconciled with the view that a painting is a cryptogram, or some kind of code. There is, of course, a lot more about illusion in Gombrich, and in many places his views about the intrusion of illusion are in no way obscure, eccentric or objectionable. For instance, a painter who makes use of the Spreading Effect, or a configuration like the Frazer Spiral, will be making use of illusions in his pictures. Op Art would be a case in point. However, it would be hasty to suppose that because some painting clearly relies on such techniques that these techniques are involved in all painting. The intrusion of illusion can act differently depending upon the context. For instance, we can say of the Frazer Spiral that concentric circles are made to look like a picture of a spiral. The illusion is the illusion of a picture of a spiral and not an illusion of spiral. On the other hand, the use of the Speading Effect produces an illusion of, for example, a lighter blue, not, that is, an illusion of a picture of a lighter blue. In responding to this illusion in a picture we may not respond with the judgment 'a lighter blue', but within a particular context we might respond 'the shape recedes there'. That its pictorial effect might not be that of our responding in an automatic way to the illusion as we do when we are dealing with its illustration in *Art and Illusion*. Illusion is often involved, then, in very obvious ways. How these specific intrusions are to be reconciled with the crypto-gram idea is something which needs to be made clear. How-ever, there is a more pressing question. It concerns the more general way in which Gombrich thinks of illusion entering into representational painting. This view would seem to be clearly incorrect. What precisely is wrong with it?

In all cases of optical illusion the situation is describable as one in which there is some x which is like y which it is not. For instance, there is a straight stick in water which is like a bent stick, which it is not, or there is a refraction of light waves which is like an oasis there now, which it is not. This is not, of course, a suffecient condition for the operation of an illusion, but it is necessary. This condition is not met where the media is supposed to give an illusion of a picture. It is inaccurate to describe the situation in a representational painting as one in which the medium looks like a picture of x, which it is not. In illusions not only is it the case that there is some x looking like some y which it is not, but there is no y in thevisual field, or if there was it would be distinguishable from the y which x looked like. In the case of the picture there most certainly is a picture there. We have a situation in which the medium is the picture, not a situation in which the medium can be said to look like the picture. The situation is the same as that in which we say that x is both a collection of atoms and a solid table. Certainly the picture is not an illusion. Wollheim is correct to state that appreciation of a picture involves (often) simul-taneous attention to texture and configuration, medium and picture, but the fact that there are some pictures for which this is not possible should not lead us to the view that the picture must then be illusory, given that the medium is not. There are lots of situations in which, from certain points of view, we learn only certain facts about an object, whereas other facts about the object have to be learnt from other points of view. For instance, from a distance one can make the judgment 'this is a pink wall', on closer or nearer inspection one can make the judgment 'there are small indentations in the surface of this wall'. The latter judgment one could not make from a dis-tance. This does not lead us to hold that the latter judgment is only possibly because of the intrusion of some illusion. We are not led to this conclusion in this case so why in the case of picture and medium? The cases are identical.

Clearly pictures are not illusory. I think for Gombrich the switch from seeing it as paint to seeing it as picture guarantees illusion. I am not sure that being faced with an exact analysis of 'illusion' Gombrich would feel disturbed to learn it cannot guarantee illusion. The niceties of the word 'illusion', I suspect, are not very much within his scope. His main contention is that under certain conditions we transcend the physical material and see a picture. *Art and Illusion* is about the conditions under which we do this. We are told that as painters or 'beholders' we have to learn to use the medium (according to rules, conventions, etc.) to make a picture out of it. It is in this account that Gombrich can be held to a conventionalist theory. The adequacy of this theory is challenged by Wollheim's argument. However, the details of the theory must be conceded as Gombrich brings forward enough puzzling cases to make this possible. Thus, the seeing of figure on ground is not so automatic a thing as we might think. The Royalist print from the French Revolution (illustration 190 in *Meditations on a Hobbyhorse*[42]) makes this very clear. Seeing that x looks like y involves seeing it that way, and certainly Gombrich is right to point out that seeing it that way presupposes a lot.

We might object, putting aside the case of *trompe-l'oeil*, that even the notion of transcending the medium was distorting. This objection brings me to what I take to be the basic insight in Gombrich's theory. This objection is not meant as a generalisation of Wollheim's contention that often we attend simultaneously both to the picture and its texture. Wollheim's point is sensitive to features of aesthetic appraisal, the objection I am thinking of points to non-aesthetic features in our perception of pictures. When we look at a picture we see the paint of which it is composed. Moreover, we know we see the paint, not as the case in which we know there is paint there and that we are looking at it only we cannot see it is paint, but as in the case where we can see it is paint. It is being able to see the paint which is one factor which immediately convinces us that we are looking at a painting. Why then should we speak of transcending the medium? This is to say why should we

speak of a shift from seeing it as paint to seeing it as picture,
when seeing it as picture involves seeing it as paint? To answer
this it is useful to bear in mind the kind of painting which is
central in *Art and Illusion*, namely the kind of representational painting which gives us something looking like a three-
dimensional world (there is a sense in which an Egyptian
painting looks like a three-dimensional world, but such a
painting does not *look* three dimensional). For the person
making such a painting, or for the observer seeing it being
constructed, it is very apparent that in the initial stages one is
only aware of a variety of paint. Almost incredibly a particular
brushstroke or mark can transform the whole into giving the
impression of, for example, a solid object, i.e. something with
a three-dimensional look.

It is at this point that one cannot change back to seeing it as
one did before. One can still see the paint, i.e. see that it is
paint at the same time as attending to what now is a picture,
but one cannot see it as just paint. In seeing the picture one
sees paint looking like a solid object, and one cannot rid
oneself of this perception. It is to this phenomenon that
Gombrich directs our attention. Nothing illusory confronts
us, but we are forced to transcend the medium. To transcend
the medium is to see x looks like y, and not to be able to resist
seeing x in this way. One still sees x, i.e. the paint, but in
seeing the paint one sees it looking like y, one cannot see just
the paint. This is a fact about looking at the kind of representational painting Gombrich is concerned with. In looking at
such painting one can see it is not y from the point of view at
which x looks like y, thus one does see that x looks like y, i.e.
one is actually seeing x *is looking* like y and so, of course, one
sees x; there is then no illusion, whereas in contrast with the
straight stick in water one cannot see from the point at which
the illusion operates that the stick is not bent, thus one cannot
see that it is a straight stick. To see a picture of y is to see some
x looking like y; a picture is something looking like something
else which it, i.e. the something, is not.

At this point it is necessary to strike out in a different
direction. What is it for one thing to look like another in the
way a painting looks like what it is a painting of? How is it that
one painting may look more like what it is a painting of than

another? Certainly Gombrich supplies a complex answer to these questions. He refers to the x looking like y, in the case of the painting, as an illusion and it is this phenomenon he tries to explain. Illusion is the thing to be explained and conventions the explanation of it. Illusion incorrectly characterises pictures, and, following Wollheim, the conventionalist theory is an inadequate explanation. However, the extent to which the conventionalist theory is held by Gombrich to be the full answer is unclear. Certainly, he is committed to the view that the hobbyhorse becomes a hobbyhorse through its use, yet against this it is his view that that which does not look very much like a female fish can serve to attract the male.[43] The general point is that conventions play a greater part in arriving at a judgment about 'looks like' than we may realise, but it is not claimed conventions fully explain what it is for one thing to look like another. Thus, Gombrich seems to say the Constable looks more like the park than the child's copy does, but that this does not mean that Constable's painting is free of conventions. The conclusion must be either Gombrich tries but fails to explain representation, or accepts there is something primitive about representation but sets out to show how, in the history of representational painting, representation has been modified by other factors. I am more inclined to think the second of these alternatives is Gombrich's thesis. One way or another an independent enquiry is necessary.

The necessity depends upon wanting to explain 'looks like' or ' "looks like" in representation'. At first view this project need not be taken on. To show paintings are 'as if' objects it might seem enough to show that we have to speak of paintings in terms of 'looks like' relationships, and thus it might seem it is not necessary to explain 'looks like' in representation. But if 'looks like' can be analysed out as a use we make of something, or as something for which we set up conventional rules, then the claim that the painting/sculpture is an 'as if' object will be very different from what I intended.

To begin with a simple statement of what is involved. To say x looks like y is to say x resembles y in looks, i.e. they have looks in common. This is no solution until 'looks' has been explained. Certainly it must not be explained to suggest that the more identical features one can establish between x and y the more like each other x and y will look. What explanation is given must accommodate the truth that paintings, for which numerous identical features may be found between them and their subjects, often do not look as like the subjects as paintings for which fewer identical features can be found. This point can be made in a more Gombrich-like fashion thus: paintings which provide more information about the subject are often judged less like the subject than paintings which provide less information. Clearly, Gombrich would not agree that a painting provides more information about its subject than another because it has more features in common with the subject than the other picture. It is Gombrich's account of this situation that the present explanation is meant to supersede.

A word of caution is needed here. The truth, as indicated above, should perhaps hold only in the form that persons think that for some paintings more identical features can be found in common with their subjects than for other paintings which, nevertheless, they hold to look more like their subjects. It may be a fact that the paintings thought to have less identical features in common with their subjects, yet which look more like their subjects, yield in fact more identical features, or alternatively more information. It may be that our vocabulary is more developed in some areas than in others, thus, we may, in some areas, more easily frame propositions to state the information content of a painting than in other areas. Or, to put the point differently, certain areas of information are more readily and fully stateable than others, and this might tempt us to think that a painting, which provides us with information of this character, provides us with more information than a painting which does not provide information that is so readily stateable. It is being assumed that one can take in that which one cannot easily express and that this may be dependent upon the public language being rarely used to express what is understood in such experiences.

For x to look like y then, x and y must have look(s) in common. The problem next becomes as difficult as the complexity of things we may refer to as 'looks which things have in common'. This concept is not easily limited by pointing to the kinds of things which count as looks, because anything perceivable (i.e. observation through sight) may count as a look things have in common. Further, looks in common are not exhausted by the visual properties of things where this is taken to mean the colour and shape of things. A book has looks but is not a look. The yellow patch on the wall may be one of the looks in common between wall and the painting of it, yet we may speak of the yellow patch as having looks. We do not say 'the yellow patch on the wall is one of the wall's looks', though we would more easily say 'the yellow patches are some of the looks which painting and wall have in common'. Similarly, we say 'John and Ralph's noses are looks they have in common' but do not say 'John's nose is one of his looks', though in giving an account of John's looks we mention his nose, or can do. Thus, a book may be one of the looks two bookshelves have in common, but it is still not a look.

To refer to a look we have to talk about a top-heavy look (looks top heavy), delicate look (looks delicate), dishonest look (looks dishonest). An x-look being a look of a thing which may be a look it has in common with other things. The same may be said of a probing look, piercing look, accusing look, though 'look' here has a different sense. The ways in which we may look at things can constitute part of what is meant by our looks and, of course, not all of our looks involve us in looking.

Where things have perceivable items in common, it follows they have looks in common. Things having looks in common do not necessarily look like each other. 'Looks like' indicates a degree of verisimilitude. This degree of verisimilitude is not attained, necessarily, through objects having a specifiable number of looks in common. Two objects may have only one or two looks in common but be held to look alike or look like each other. There are occasions when we can say of two women that they look like each other through some specifiable look they have in common, for instance, the impression they give that they survey everything with a puzzled stare. In such a case we may have to specify the look in common more carefully or specifically than this, which is to say we may have to describe the look more precisely than it appears under the description 'a puzzled stare'. This is not to say, however, that the look in question would need to be broken down into a number of observable features which, in virtue of so being,

could all be accredited looks in common. It would be philis-
tine to suppose that the looks would be more accurately
signified by a description of colours, tones and shapes. As a
matter of fact looks are recognisable, though the more ato-
mistic descriptions would not be recognised as applying.
Thus, a look can be exhibited by dissimilar structures. In
other words, the look in common, justifying the looks like
assertion, can be apprehended as a primitive resemblance.
The appropriate degree of verisimilitude is attained not
through numerous looks in common but through the looks in
common being of a certain category. They need to be salient
characteristics of the things looking like each other. An
instuctive analogy is the case of metaphor. The cognitive
content of the metaphor is apprehendable in realising the
salient characteristics of one, or other, of the things implied
by the metaphor to be in the relation of resemblance. Though
a cup and an ink bottle are physical objects one cannot
construct the metaphor 'this ink bottle is my cup'. Being a
physical object is not a salient characteristic of cups. Blackness and density are salient characteristics of ink, despite ink
being purchasable in many colours and densities, and for this
reason it is possible to construct the metaphor 'my nightmares
are whirlpools of ink'; dense blackness being a quality appro-
priately attributable to nightmares. Those salient characteristics of things, which are perceivable items of those things, are
the sorts of things things must have in common to look like
each other. Naturally, the nearer one comes to producing a
copy of something then the nearer one comes to capturing the
salient characteristics of that thing, and it is for this reason
that those paintings, of which it is commonly held that they
have many attributes in common with their subjects, are said
to look very much like their subjects. This is not to say that
paintings can ever be copies of what they are paintings,
though this is not so for Gombrich's reason that the alleged
looks in common can never be looks in common in fact.
Rather, it is because a painting is not the same kind of thing as
that of which it is a painting, though it can have looks in
common with its subject. A copy of a book is another book, a
copy of a £1 note will not necessarily be a £1 note, but this is
institutionally decided, and has to be set against the possibility

of the two pieces of paper being identical. Numerous correspondences will, at a certain point, yield salient appearances or
rather yield them in some form. Painters trying for many
correspondences, if successful, do not paint representational
paintings.

It is possible now to detail how some paintings, providing
fewer correspondences than others look more like their subjects than those with which they are compared, and, because
of this feature of looking more like, yield more information
about their subjects than the others. This can be so for at
least two of the reasons we can give in arguing that one
account is more informative than another. Firstly, it may be so
because the information we can derive we judge to be of
greater importance than that derivable from the work containing more correspondences. Secondly, it can be so because
the essential propositions necessary for stating accurately
what look the picture and its subject have in common can be
more numerous than with the picture containing more correspondences. The distinction being sought in this second
point is better conveyed in illustration. A yellow, square
object may be represented in a picture by a yellow, square
shape, but the yellowness of this object, as the peculiar
yellowness it is, may not be represented. There can be a
correspondence of yellow without a correspondence of the
special yellow character of the object. To specify this special
character of the object we may need to speak of shade, tone,
emotive force, etc. A painting that concerned itself mainly
with a presentation of such yellowness may be more informative of its subject than some other painting that presents more
correspondences but not one of them so precisely.

This correspondence between objects explains 'looks like'
in a general way, but it is insufficient for making the distinction between neutral and magnetic 'as if' states of affairs, and
a picture fits into the latter category. For this reason, Wollheim's view in *Art and its objects* that resemblance will not
explain representation because the explanation must begin at
the point of 'seeing as', is correct. Seeing that x and y have
looks in common is not necessarily the same thing as seeing x
as y. It was this point, though made in a more general way, to
which attention was drawn earlier where it was said that the

magnetic 'as if' situation involved thinking of x as y, whereas
this was not involved in the neutral situation. However, it
would be wrong to conclude that resemblance may be ommit-
ted in an explanation of representation, because it *is resemblance in special contexts* which explains why two copies of the
same book do not involve seeing the one as the other, and why
the painted material has to be *seen as* Dylan Thomas in John's
portrait. Part of the special context surrounding resemblance
in representation is that the resemblance is one between
different kinds of things. The various copies of a book are not
emptied of their interest for us when we have consumed the
fact of them all looking like each other, whereas the x looking
like y, which is the painting, is without interest if we are not
concerned with its resemblance. The painting, the sculpture is
a different kind of thing from what it as a painting or sculpture
of. It is for this reason that you cannot do a painting of another
painting, except in the sense that you can do a painting of a
context in which a painting is present; the best you can achieve
will be a copy. The important thing about x, in the situation of
its looking like y, where this is the situation of a picture being
present, is just the fact of x looking like y. It is this perception
of x that becomes irresistible, and it is this fact that Gombrich
attempts to illuminate. It is not just the fact of resemblance
which explains representation but the fact of resemblance
being the limit of our interest in one of the things in the
relation of resemblance. Certain objects, objects like paintings, are especially made to make this limiting of our interest
easy. To be able to concentrate on the resemblance to the
exclusion of all else is to see the one thing as the other. In the
relation *x looks like y* it follows that y looks like x, 'looks like'
exhibits this degree of symmetry, but though x looking like y
may involve us in being able to see x as y it does not follow that
we must then be able to see y as x. We may see John looks like
his father, and, at times, through a special focusing of our
attention, we may be able to see John as his father, and yet we
may find that the father stubbornly refuses to be seen as John.
In this case we may say that what the father is, apart from a
person resembling his son, prevents our focusing purely on
this fact of resemblance about him. Wollheim thinks that we
cannot say of Napoleon that he resembles some drawing made

of him, though we may say that the drawing resembles him. For Wollheim this is offered as fairly conclusive evidence that resemblance in representation is being used in some special sense. However, Wollheim is confusing our not being able to see Napoleon as the drawing with the claim that Napoleon resembles the drawing. The former claim is most likely to be true, but does not undermine the symmetry of the resemblance between the pencil marks and Napoleon. Moreover, we must be careful not to be misled by the way in which purpose and effect attach themselves to assertions of likeness, for we may feel that the purpose we had in mind, and the effect we produce through asserting x is like y, is something which, if it should get transposed to the assertion y is like x, would be inappropriate, but this should not make us doubt the symmetry of the relationship. To say of some aspiring writer that he writes like Proust may be to attempt to criticise him through a claim about his derivatory style, but because we have this in mind in comparing him with Proust this is no reason for having it in mind when we see that, because we have asserted that he is like Proust, we must allow that Proust writes like the aspiring writer. Wollheim holds that resemblance cannot explain representation because someone who was ignorant of the practice of representation would be unable to see the resemblance between painting and what it was a painting of; but is this to say anymore than that we have to learn to see how objects of different kinds can resemble each other? This is just as true of objects of the same kind. It is a special feat to teach a child that two identical cups look like each other. Resemblance is not something which is understood immediately.

As an incidental point it can be noted that we are in a postion to accommodate certain developments in contemporary visual art. A painting and a piece of sculpture will be magnetic 'as if ' objects, but this allows for the possibility of constructing magnetic 'as if ' objects which enable us to see them as paintings or pieces of sculpture when they are not. Pieces of sculpture may be made that have to be seen in a painterly way (e.g. they seem to employ the illusionistic devices of paintings), and objects may be placed in special contexts like galleries where they give the appearance of being pieces of sculpture, thus we will have something which is *as if* it was a painting, and something which is *as if* it was a piece of sculpture.

As a word of warning the account I have been offering has not been meant as a unique characterisation of what a painting is, for instance, nothing has been said to explain the distinction between sculpture and painting, but more than this the account has not been offered as a complete explanation of what is to count as a representation, even where this notion is being used in a very general sense. It has been my intention rather to bring out those features of representations which Gombrich's account denies, and to say enough to make it clear that representations do possess these features.

At this point there are two things which need to be done. One is to relate this explanation of representation to our ordinary talk about pictures. The other is to return to Gombrich by a different route, and the reason for this is that the explanation as it has been advanced conflicts with an as yet unmentioned aspect of Gombrich's views.

It has been advanced that a picture of y is the situation of there being something which is not y being like y in looks. It is to this situation we refer in speaking of a picture of y. The something which is not y but is like y in looks can be paint, plastic material, sand, sea shells, bits of rope, pencil marks, pastel, etc. Expressing this fact by using the words 'looks like' is unusual in English, instead we use the words 'representation', 'picture', 'painting', etc. 'Looks like' is a locution used in our talk about pictures, but normally its function is not that of being included as part of the explanation of our concept of a picture. We say of the photograph 'this looks like John', we may say of the portrait by Augustus John 'this looks very much like Dylan Thomas'. In the former case we are judging the photograph to be of John, in the latter case we are judging the degree of verisimilitude achieved. In saying of something that it is a painting, or a representation, we are indicating there is something which is like in looks something which it is not. We may be unable to specify very precisely what this something is, but we will know that it is something other than the something it looks like. To confront paintings is to confront magnetic 'as if' situations, whereas to confront John's father, whom he resembles, is not to. We may fail to be involved with the 'as if' object as an 'as if' object, i.e. we may fail to see we are confronted with a picture; the culture we come from may explain a failure of this sort. Nevertheless, it is a special kind of fact about a picture that it is an 'as if' object. It is singled out in our language as being an 'as if' object. this is what the word 'picture' does. Its primary function as an artefact is to work as an 'as if' object. It is an incidental fact about John's father that he looks like someone he is not, it is a central fact about a picture, for a picture is something which is like in looks to that which it is not.

One thread, in the account I have been giving, needs exploration. A painting would be judged without controversy to be representational, though what it was a painting of did not exist nor ever had. Yet we may be unable to specify what it is which looks like something other than it is. We may be in the position of having to say that something (in a darkened room it may be ambiguous whether or not coloured material, e.g. luminous paint, or a play of light confronts us, 'something coloured' may be as near as we can get) has looks in common with something which does not exist, which the rather indefinite something clearly enough is not. In confronting a representation our position may be that of not knowing whether or not the something (which the something, we know not what very definitely, looks like) exists, but knowing there *is* something, which looks like that something, whether or not it exists. Moreover, in this situation we are compelled to see the something (the something that we know not what very definitely) as looking like the something which may or may not exist; this is how we apprehend this something.

But doesn't saying 'x looks like y means x and y have looks in common' entail that checking the correspondences between x and y must be discovering the truth value of 'x looks like y'? If we could never check on the correspondences between x and y because y has not existed nor will, the does it make sense to talk of 'looks in common'? An amendment seems to help, namely, 'x looks like y' means 'if y then x will have looks in common with it' and 'if not y then x would have looks in common with it if it was, and it is logically possible for it to be'. Thus, seeing x looks like y involves seeing that y is a possibility.

The next problem is epistemological. How are we able to
apprehend that x and y would have looks in common? An
alternative formulation is, what directs us to y in claiming x
looks like y? Another alternative is, what makes us apprehend
there is something looking like something it is not, where the
first something is experienced but may not be understood as
anything over and above something looking like something it
is not, and where the second something may never have been
given in experience, and perhaps is not givable anyway? What
is given to experience and what is apprehendable as such is the
image, the picture, but the analysis is that the picture *is* just
the state of affairs of something looking like something it is
not.

There are several aspects to removing this problem.

Without the background for pictures we may fail to see the
picture. We may apprehend the object as coloured material
only. Normally, to see the picture involves coming into the
situation looking for looks like relationships, and it is a fact
that sometimes we do so without being in a position to
compare actual correspondences. The claim then is that there
is an epistemological problem. The Gombrich account by
implication denies there is this problem. Shortly it will be
shown that Gombrich's account confuses representations
with cases which are quite distinct.

If we may knowingly create a likeness to something that
goes beyond our experience then we can knowingly apprehend this likeness. To knowingly confront a picture is to be
committed to exercising one's ability to see likeness. One
searches for what it is a picture of. We have the ability to see
that there could be a world like that. There must be the
possibility of there being new situations in the world for us,
and we can apprehend their newness. If we apprehend newness there is no logical barrier to our apprehending a likeness
to what if it *was* would be new. If there is a likeness this is a
good reason for our seeing it. The apprehension that the
subject of a picture is a member of a new class of objects is an
unlikely experience. Typically, the subject of pictures concerns that particular, the concrete. We do believe we apprehend the particular in a picture though we have no experience
of the particular.

An empiricist account of how and what we can apprehend gives rise to the epistemological problem. The argument against the empiricist-creation theory in chapter 2, with the necessary transpositions, is the kind of argument needed to dispel the problem. That the problem does not arise anyway is evidenced by our conviction that in our experience of painting we confront pictures of particulars which transcend out experiences.

For Gombrich questions about the identification of the image do not involve questions about correspondences. This is his positive theory about seeing representations. I noted previously that he occasionally seems to use a primitive view of 'looks like' instead. His positive theory is that we transcend the medium by means of conventions; we agree tacitly to use the medium as something other than it is. There are things Gombrich's theory explains but they are not representations. This confusion of representations with cases which are quite distinct shows Gombrich does not have a theory about representation.

Consider the difference between seeing ∴ as a k and seeing (⌣) as a face. In both cases there is likely to be a switch in readings ('readings' here being used metaphorically). With k we are too used to it to see anything other than k (the letter). In both cases in my experience, you often have to prod the viewer, 'it's a k', 'it's a face'. 'Oh, I see,' is the response. In the first case the arrangement of dots is transcended in applying the convention that anything with that sort of shape counts as the letter k, or can be made to count as such. It is not that the arrangement of dots is an 'as if' object looking like a k but not being one, the arrangement of dots is a k and there are flexible rules that establish this. In the second case we reach the interpretation of the thing as a face not by seeing that some convention establishes that this is a face, but in seeing that these marks have looks in common with faces, or could have looks in common with a face. Gombrich's account of representation explains the dots case (not a case of representation), but fails to explain the face case.

But what leads Gombrich away from 'matching' or from what he would probably consider a crude common-sense view of the matter? Are there theoretical considerations on which he is relying?

Gombrich opposes the theory of the innocent eye: the theory that perception is basically a seeing and cognition of coloured patches that the painter, who is to capture nature, must record or copy on his canvas. Gombrich's view of perception is Popperian. Perceiving is guessing at something out there, it is framing an hypothesis and setting about testing it. The view is allied to that of the world being merely an interpretation. Gombrich sees the innocent eye theory of artistic creation as the theory behind Impressionism, and one the Impressionists tried to paint in accordance with. They were trying to paint the image on the retina before conceptualisation. Gombrich is right to see this as primitive psychology. There can be no such thing as a copy of the image on the retina where one is supposed to be copying what it is one is aware of before one has conceptualised it. However, there is nothing in this opposition to the innocent eye theory to deny that one can see one's environment as a collection of coloured patches (art students are sometimes urged to do this and there is nothing unintelligible in the suggestion) or to deny that one can try to produce an object that has looks in common with this collection. This is not the same as saying the painter should try to produce a collection of coloured patches that are identical with the coloured patches he has given himself as the subject of his picture. Gombrich is right to make us realise that, within a certain context, it would not work to use the exact shade and colour of whatever it is one is painting. But this is because it is the look which must correspond and not what is there; it is not because things do not or cannot have looks in common. Gombrich's view appears to be that painting cannot be just matching, because there is nothing there to match (it is true that he does not hold consistently to this theory for he allows matching after making, but the structure of his argument appears to be: making must precede matching because there is nothing to match, the artist is forced to make; or is it that: if there is something to match one couldn't match it anyway?) but this does not follow from it being impossible to paint the deconceptualised experience, it is not even clear that it follows from all perceptions being interpretations.

If the kind of representational painting which concerns Gombrich can be accounted for in terms of 'as if' objects, in the sense meant, what should we say of painting which Gombrich would consider non-representational? Earlier I referred to Wollheim's loosening our concept of representation in *On Drawing an Object* and in *Art and its Objects*. Stokes in *Reflections on the Nude*[44] reads Wollheim as saying that it is difficult to prevent even the simplest marks on two-dimentional surfaces from being open to representational interpretations. It is to this point Wollheim refers in *Art and its Objects* in speaking of the pervasiveness of representational seeing.[45] Thus, we can see a black stroke on an empty white canvas as a slit in the canvas, or as something in front of the canvas concealing smaller surfaces in other colours. Such descriptions of the black stroke on white are descriptions of an 'as if' object. A quibble about the word 'representational' can be set aside here, it will be enough to argue that the kind of interest we take to paintings (all visual art objects is really the point) is only explained if the interest is at least in part an interest in them as 'as if' objects. Transmuted, Wollheim's point can be stated as: it is difficult to prevent even the simplest marks on a two-dimensional surface ('simplest marks' would be sufficient) being open to interpretation as an 'as if' object or objects. To clarify this claim, in its initial formulation, it is as much about what we do as what it is possible to do. There is no argument showing that a representational interpretation must always be possible. What needs to be argued, however, is that an interest in the painting as an 'as if' object is necessary to our interest in it as painting. Wollheim's point transmuted is only that an 'as if' reading will be hard to resist. I need to argue for the necessity of this interest in painting so as to extend my account of the 'as if' entering art. I shall argue this in two ways. Firstly, I shall try to show how we move naturally into talk about the 'as if' when we are trying to describe what we are looking at in confronting an abstract ('non-representational') work. Secondly, I shall discuss critically an alternative way of accounting for our experiences in front of works of this type.

What interests in, or ways of seeing, a painting can be discounted as having nothing to do with seeing it as a painting (i.e. being concerned with it as a painting)? It might be suggested that just as there could be no specifiable limit to

what interests we bring to painting, so there could be no
specifiable limit to irrelevant interests in painting. Alternatively, it might be suggested that no interest in painting could
be logically barred, for the subject depended upon the nature
of painting and this would be in a state of flux. I will maintain
certain interests are irrelevant necessarily and that certain
other interests are relevant necessarily.

Suppose a detective is following me around the Pitti Palace
in Florence. My holiday with my mistress is being observed at
my wife's instructions. The detective has taken with him an
apprentice who has to be instructed in my appearance. Ac-
cordingly, the apprentice is directed to a large canvas to his
left. The intention is that he should locate myself and mistress
standing in front of the picture. Suppose the picture is Reuben's *The Outbreak of War*. There is no necessity that he
should know anything about the picture, over and above its
location and size, in order to be able to fasten onto his
principle subjects. Obviously this crude though efficient identification of an object has nothing to do with taking on *The
Outbreak of War* as a picture.

Suppose, following a war between ourselves and aliens
from space, the victorious aliens begin to subject certain of
our artefacts to chemical analysis and one such object is
Reuben's picture. The descriptions produced may be very
detailed, not only telling what substances were found but also
how and in what quantities they were distributed. The descriptions of the substances are likely to make use of colour and
textural descriptions. Again, obviously, this interest in the
picture would have nothing to do with taking in the object as a
picture. This would be so even if the chemical analysis yielded
a story about the physical processes that gave rise to *The
Outbreak of War*.

The situation is not changed if the picture is not Reuben's
but Pollock's. Probably, at the level of philosophical reflection, we are not clear about our concept of physical object. If
the cases I have described are fairly central examples of an
interest in objects as physical objects, then it may be sensible
to maintain that an interest in a painting must be something
over and above an interest in it as a physical object. The
anarchist tendencies of artists need not conclusively settle

things here. If an artist maintains that his object in his work is to produce an object which is irrevocably and primarily a physical object, and that illusionistic properties have been deliberately expelled, it is at least open to us to be sceptical as to the possibility of the achievement, and if there was success to find no interest in the object, though we might admit to an interest in *anything* that was a painting. In other words, the act of doing and then calling by a name is something we can make mistakes about. A painting could not necessarily be, for instance, that which results from acts of painting.

In *Art and its Objects* Wollheim argues that physical objects can have expressive properties, and that it is not always the case that things we see as being expressive we could or can see in any other way. The inference would seem to be that to perceive the expressive properties of a thing is to perceive that thing as a physical object. However, at the same time, Wollheim thinks to respond to the expressive properties is to have a physiognomic perception of the object. 'When we endow a natural object or an artefact with expressive meaning we tend to see it corporeally; that is, we tend to credit it with a particular look which bears a marked analogy to some look that the human body wears and that is constantly conjoined with an inner state.'[46] This account is meant to cover both 'natural' and 'correspondence' expression (this distinction is Wollheim's). This account is not in direct opposition to the account being given, because, despite certain Humean undertones which I feel unhappy about, it seems to bring us back to representational seeing. Wollheim does not explicitly connect his claim about the pervasiveness of representational seeing with his thesis about the apprehension of expressive properties, but the latter turns out to be an illustration of the former, or in the case of painting it seems to be.

This is not the end of the matter, for Wollheim also argues that physical objects can have representational properties, and so again the inference would seem to be that to apprehend the representational properties is to apprehend the object as a physical object. 'it ... seems absurd to insist that representational seeing, and the judgements to which it characteristically gives rise, implicitly presuppose a denial of the physicality both of the representation itself and that on which it lies.'[47]

Thus, the claim that to perceive a painting involves seeing it as something over and above a physical object remains contested. However, this opposition is not worrying. If it is correct it means that the notion of physical object I was working with was too limited, but also, if it is correct, it means that there is no reason given for supposing that apprehension of a painting, as a painting, is not or can not be a matter of apprehending it as an 'as if' object.

These considerations from *Art and its Objects* bring me to a point about the naturalness and ease with which we begin to talk about so called non-representational abstract work in 'as if' terms. We may attribute depth to the picture plane, we may insist on a physiognomic reading, we may speak of elements in the picture threatening, fondling, keeping aloof, from other elements. The suggestion is that we do deal with what confronts us as an 'as if' world. The arrangement of physical material in the painting is not a situation in which one piece of material actually threatens another, or if this was so the event would be of quite another order, as when, say, a hanging shelf of heavy granite threatens the girders of a bridge. The physical material rather gives the impression of there being forces, having a life of their own, that can threaten, expel, fondle, etc., other elements in the picture.

The kind of 'as if' descriptions which we can give are as diverse as the kind of 'as if' objects about which they will be. None of this is to say that it should be typical of our attitude in front of an abstract painting to work towards some *firm* 'as if' reading of it. The overpowering nature of the experience may seem diminished by formulating a succinct 'as if' description of the elements involved in our experience. There is something insensitive about being instantly articulate in front of any painting. The important thing is to look and to dwell. The experience is not one of coming to a conclusion, as though that was what it was all about, what is important is having the experience. It is in the nature of the experience that we regard what confronts us as an 'as if' world or worlds. The elements may be shifting constantly. When we put the emphasis on the red, the yellow recedes, when we put the emphasis on the blue, the red and yellow obstruct us like road-signs. Against this flux it will seem false that there is an 'as if' description which describes how it is when we take on the picture, but this attitude is really consistent with the thesis. In so-called representational works certain easy and straightforward 'as if' descriptions will be undeniable, but it would be correct to feel that they did not get very close to what the experience in front of such paintings is like. The special world we compose out of our experience of *Las Meninas* is something much more than the description of certain persons watching, or being painted by, Velasquez, and any description is likely to seem inappropriate. It is not surprising that unique and special experiences are felt to be unrepresentable and indescribable, unless, that is, writing and painting are serious activities for us.

But it might be objected that I am neglecting either (a) 'it is a deep reddish blue with yellow specks on and I like that, I find it satisfying' or following Sibley, (b) 'it is lovely, pretty, dainty, very graceful and delicate'[48], or both.

What I have in mind by (a) is that school of thought, possibly originating from a simple-minded conception of a psychological investigation into perception of aesthetically desirable objects, which holds that it is some brute fact about many human beings that certain shapes, colours and textures are liked by them. Thus, the complete answer to the question 'Why does he like that picture?' might be 'Because that shade of blue, used extensively in the picture, is his favourite, he likes it.' That psychologists are prepared to think they can explain, from a psychologist's point of view, aesthetic experience in something like this way is clear from H. J. Eysenck's chapter on psychology and aesthetics in *Sense and Nonsense in Psychology*.[49] What there is in this account which is an objection to my own is that certain properties, which I would accept as physical properties, are liked or disliked for being themselves, and that it is searching for such things to like that explains our interest in painting, or explains *an* interest which is an interest in painting as painting. On this account a painting can be conceived of as an artefact with specific physical properties which are intended to be admired. The account does not rule out necessarily other separate interests we might have in painting. It does not even have to make the claim that what it gives an account of is something present in all paintings, though it would accord with the aim to give a scientific account to attempt comprehensiveness.

There are two objections to this account.

To begin with, the selection of a visual route to an artefact's physical properties (or if we extend the experimental psychologist's account to music, then the selection of a visual or auditory route to an artefact's or performance's physical properties) seems in virtue of what kind of account the account is, arbitrary. If it can be a brute fact about one that one likes a certain shade of yellow, then it can be a brute fact that one likes a certain temperature for the water in one's bath, or for the central heating in one's home, or that one likes an animal with a silky coat, or that one likes the property whisky has to produce a warming sensation as it goes down. But this selection of hypothesised brute facts about one is not a selection from one's aesthetic dispositions. If the account is supposed to give an explanation of our typical concerns with paintings as paintings, and if it conceives of this explanation as one about our aesthetic interests, then it is hard to see how it could not imply an extension of the aesthetic area to cover a range of sensations promoted by the physical properties of things that we find ourselves liking or disliking. An alternative would be to produce an analysis of the kind of liking involved that was more informative than it being a liking of a certain shade of yellow. But it is difficult to see how this would be possible without providing a deeper analysis of what was liked about the shade of yellow. This investigation might well lead away from the suggestion that a certain colour was liked simply for being that colour and that this was a brute fact about the person liking it.

But it might be maintained that this objection is not to the point. That it is difficult to see how such an account can claim to be unique to the aesthetic area is not to say that it is not an account of how we can respond to paintings, (treating them in the process as paintings). It is not my intention to characterise the aesthetic area, but merely to show how the 'as if' must enter into our transactions with the objects of visual art. This brings me to my second and more relevant objection, which is that I do not believe we like colours, shapes and textures simply for them being the colours, shapes and textures which they are. No doubt, we can ask people questions in experimental environments about their preferences and they will give us answers. No doubt, we may find that at the level of simple examples there will be amongst the test group wide agreement in their preferences. It may also be possible to correlate the majority's score with that of attested experts on good taste, so as to purport to discover whether or not the majority have good taste. But clearly, whether or not the investigation can proceed further, we *must* ask 'what is it about this shade of yellow that you like?'. It may well be that the statement 'this person likes being confronted with this shade of yellow' says nothing about what his interest is in this situation, and, at best, is something we may correlate with what he really attends to. More positively, it is not so unlikely that the person asked why he liked a particular shade of yellow will explain away his liking by what he can associate the shade with, and thus by what he turns the shade into. The shade may seem as the morning sky in Italy suffused with light, or more likely, something less concrete and more ambiguous. It might be said that such explanations are only forthcoming against incitement to say what the shade is like, but it is arguable that what the shade is like is just how the shade is apprehended as something attractive to contemplate. That a person might not readily provide this explanation could well, as in the case above, be attributed to the indefiniteness of the 'as if ' experience, one for which a precise enough reference did not seem available. This kind of explanation offers a greater chance of our concern with visual properties being made self-explanatory than is possible with the idea that it is a brute fact about us that we are gripped by certain visual properties.

The new suggestion that visual properties are liked through some 'as if' perception of them, is itself not alien to experimental psychological investigation. It is something like this suggestion which Hosper's makes in his paper 'Art and Reality' in Hook's *Art and Philosophy*,[50] although the point we may infer from Gombrich, that how a certain shade is seen depends upon its context, would need to be heeded.

The list of properties in (b), above, *seem* of a different order, and set separate problems. The argument might be that these qualities are qualities of physical objects and that they make our concern with these objects self-explanatory. It would be difficult to deny that 'I like it because it is graceful, dainty and delicate' has a more understandable relationship between preference and reason than is apparent in 'I like it because it is lemon and rectangular'. On the other hand, thinking something to be graceful, dainty and delicate over-determines one's liking it and thinking it good. It is institutional that the words 'graceful', 'dainty' and 'delicate' have a commendatory function. They are not, of course, without descriptive content, though this does not allow us to stipulate necessary and sufficient conditions for something being delicate, dainty or graceful. If the descriptive content is not itself explanatory of our interest in objects possessing these qualities, then the value of these qualities, compared with that of those I was discussing, presents no alternative to the idea that concern with a painting requires paying attention to its 'as if' characteristics. In Sibley's article he gives examples of how he thinks we argue for the judgment that something is delicate or graceful. A thing will be said to be delicate because of its pale colours, because of its flecks of bright blue, a thing will be said to be graceful because of its thinness, because its outline curves slightly, because of the way the lines converge. If these are, in fact, the ways we argue for these assertions then it is clear no advance has been made in trying to produce a sphere of interest in painting as painting that absolutely excludes a concern with the 'as if'. The qualities which the descriptive contents of 'delicate' and 'graceful' direct us to are the qualities already discussed under (a). Sibley's own thesis confirms this conclusion. It is part of his argument that a statement of non-aesthetic qualities does not entail the aesthetic quality for which the statement may be offered in justification. Thus, the admission that an object has aesthetic quality a does make one admit some preference for the object, but if d is the descriptive statement offered to justify the attribution of a to the object it does not follow that a; even if a can explain the preference d cannot. As these considerations do not in themselves undermine the 'as if' status of visual art and because of all the other reasons given in this chapter, I conclude that the 'as if' is both central and necessary to an understanding of this area.

9

The 'as if' in dancing and music

In this chapter I shall very briefly consider dancing and briefly consider music.

DANCING

Why is there the need to dance? What are we trying to do? What happens to us in the dance? And how is the dance observed? What is in it for the observer?

Pathological explanations may be to hand, but what is required is an account of how the dancer sees it. It is unlikely that dancers will have formulated their consciousness of themselves as dancers. Only those, who have lived by dance, may have had need to say what is involved, as Nijinsky did.[51] From outside the dance, poets, like Yeats,[52] may try to explain the dancer, but the more typical reaction is to find it enough to be transfixed by what one sees.

For children (within our culture) dancing begins in acts that are very obviously those of pretence; the pretending done through movement. Swaying for trees, large steps for giants, rolling for balls. But such beginnings are not those of the children in the film *Black Orpheus*. Their dancing begins with music. The music encourages the movement and the movement takes them over. For our children music is initially an accompaniment. Later, the dancing is abstracted from obvious acts of pretence and tied in with certain kinds of music in socially acceptable contexts. At this stage dancing is explained partly by the social needs these contexts meet, but within this there is the undeniable love of dancing. Of course, the desire to dance is not universal, thus, for reasons connected with the history of dancing in Western civilisation, females are more likely to experience it than males, and further, it is likely to be the case that Yeats was right in thinking that the less academic one's mind the more easily and fully one could allow oneself to flow into dance activity.

121

Of course, sexual desires are fulfilled or can be, in the act of dancing. They may be fulfilled in an exhibitionist way, and perhaps, in part, this helps to explain the female's enthusiasm for dancing. They may be fulfilled in a strictly 'as if' fashion when two people simulate coitus. Even the female's exhibitionism is likely to work suggestively, thus involving her in the 'as if'. But it is a reduction of what is involved in dancing, in these very normal contexts, to see it as fully explained through sexual motivation. It is symptomatic of a mind that cannot really bring itself to think about how the participants see their activity to attempt so easy a reduction, like persons who fail to respond to pop groups attributing the enthusiasm of a largely female audience to a desire for mass masturbation.

Dancing gives the appearance of a transformation. One changes the perception of the environment. Normally the head is fairly still in observing, but it is a feature of much dancing that one's viewpoint is shifting constantly. The viewpoint does not shift in accordance with pragmatic needs, but shifts without interest in the environment. In this way the environment is opened up, one gains space. The experience is similar on the merry-go-round, where to be riding around is to feel that one hurls through some immense space dotted occasionally with a familiar face, whereas the observer merely sees people going round and round. This experience is as applicable to being swirled off one's feet in a waltz as to shaking one's head vigorously to soul music.

This feeling about the space around one is, in a sense, just a consequence of dancing, though it is something to be incorporated into the dance, in the sense that one can reach out for it, jab into it, recoil from it, turn one's back upon it, but the central thing about dancing is oneself in movement. It is not enough to move to the music, to be in rhythm. For the observer this will be enough, but this matching the movement to the music may be, for oneself, a purely mechanical activity. One could absent-mindedly dance, and so it cannot be one's intentions in that situation which explain the desire to dance, or what it is that the dance is for the dancer. The dance is magical, it is transforming. The movement allows one to seem to be another, to seem to have taken on another role. It is an activity which makes the otherwise absurd claim 'I am God'

(Nijinsky) real. The dancer, in the dance, may produce a life in its entirety. It will have its birth and death, and the life throughout will be patterned by the music, thus becoming a meaningful whole, rather than a series of random events. The dancer may be gay, or light, or tragic, or without human emotion, a force without roots in humanity (in this latter instance we have the romantic thought of the passionless face often connected with the *femme fatale*) but all of this will be *in* the dance. These moods need have nothing to do with how the dancer is as a person, they need only be things assumed in the dance, roles that the dance makes possible. To dance is to pretend to a force, magnificence and life which one could not live.

This situation is reflected in the observer's perception of the dance. The person with his limitations and boundaries sheds them as he enters the dance. At this point anything seems possible. It is like the curtain going up in the theatre, anything may transpire, but it will be only as if it did. The dance is a mask. The plain and empty person is transformed into some vibrant and dynamic force. It is interesting to reflect that Yeats was, in effect, consigning women to the world of the 'as if '.

MUSIC

There is a long-standing, theoretical dispute in music about what constitutes a correct way of listening to and talking about music. I shall not give this dispute anything like full treatment, rather I shall indicate some of the arguments which need to be answered and some of the arguments which need to be argued in order to justify my assertion about the 'as if' in music.

The theory which would be most unsympathetic to my case is the one which would confine our attention in music to its notes, in that aspect of them which is given to us through musical notation. It is not essential to the theory that the listener be able to express himself in this notation, though a thorough knowledge of music would involve the possession of this ability.

Aside from the way it is expressed (the way in which one is able to express it to oneself) interest is to be confined to things like being able to hear that one note is highter than another, that there is a key change, that the rhythm is constant throughout, etc. It is allowed that pleasure or displeasure may accompany perceptions of the music that are of this order. In some versions of the theory the pleasure will be an inexplicable brute fact, just as in a comparable theory concerning the visual arts it is supposed to be (as has been seen) a brute fact that certain shapes, colours and textures please us; on other versions, the pleasure will be dependent on the perception that such facts about the music, as those the theory urges one to attend to, indicate considerable ingenuity and inventiveness on the part of the composer. What is denied by the theory is the relevance of interpreting music as being descriptive of something, or as expressing emotion, or as having meaning, or as being an 'as if' entity itself, or as giving rise to 'as if' states. It is allowed, people come to music with these interests and appear to have them satisfied, but what is not allowed is that these interests are appropriate to music as music, or to music as a thing which can aspire to the condition of art. To be interested in the music is to be interested in the purely musical features of the music, and the purely musical features of music are judged to be the sound components out of which it is made, as those sound components are understood, or identifiable, through musical theory.

The most puzzling or obstinate feature of this account, for someone wishing to oppose it, is that anyone can think this to be a description of what is involved in listening to music. There is a psychological problem of explaining how anyone can think such a theory correct.

I think any attempt to describe the art form from the point of view of it being referential, or meaningful, or emotional, or 'as iffy' in some way, is likely to be found galling. If the experience was big enough, or overwhelming enough, and this is how people often feel about their musical experiences, then any attempt to deal with the object of the experience, or the experience itself, will be quite likely to encounter resistance. On the other hand, a description of the music at the level of musical theory will seem neutral and palatable. For some people the description will be of no significance because they cannot read music, and for those who can it will state undeniable facts about the music that can be correlated with their experiences as inspired by the music.

This characteristic can crop up in all sorts of places. For instance, having witnessed a marvellous goal, two men, without quite realising they are doing it, may compete for a description of it:

A: 'It was bloody great he did it on the twist, miles out and hit it like a rocket.'

B: 'Yes, but more than that it was with that easy swerve and effortlessness of his, just when we felt it was all over and we couldn't win.'

In these situations there is a feeling that no one can get the thing just as it was experienced, though something cold and neutral like 'he kicked it into the top right-hand corner of the goal from 40 yards out, at 60 m.p.h. with 30 seconds to go to the final whistle' is acceptable, because it correlates with something that evades description. It is within the general theory I am advancing that to cover the experience to the point that it satisfies, is to make it with the reader as if that experience is being re-lived. Nothing will do but the evocation of how it was.

In addition to this disposition to reject any description of our more overwhelming experiences, is the fact of the awfulness of many such descriptions, exhibiting, as they do, pretentiousness and rhetorical abandon. Upholders of the theory I am considering are normally only too ready to produce examples of such pieces of writing.

Here, then, we have one possible explanation of the tendency to withdraw, to confining one's talk about music to the level of musical theory. But, of course, there is nothing in this explanation to explain how, in listening to music, we might need to confine our experience to noting the musical-theory-type features of the performance, and to deriving pleasure from them.

Another element in the motivation towards this theory may concern a feeling of superiority that a person, who knows his musical theory, is likely to conceal from himself. In a television programme I watched, Hans Keller argued that the music he had been listening to was musically uninteresting to the musical ear. His ear was very good, and he was able to hear that the music never once left a certain key and that harmonically it was very simple. These things were facts, and it was suggested it followed from them, where seeing the 'deduction' had nothing to do with taste ('personal likes and dislikes') or with the fact that Keller's natural musical habitat might be with classical composers as opposed to pop performers (he had been listening to pop performers), that the music so described was uninteresting and bad. Here was an example of someone thinking that because he had the knowledge to hear more precisely how the music was made up than was possible for the majority of the audience, then some evaluation immediately followed from the factual assertions (detected by the musical ear) about the music. The implication was that anyone with a musical ear would concur. The feeling of superiority referred to is that of feeling one's own position is the right position from which to judge because one is able to analyse how the thing to be judged is made. One does not admit to this feeling of superiority; one has been led seemingly naturally to the view that one's own position is the one to judge from. Thus, the attitude is, one is not being superior, one is simply being musical.

This concealed sense of superiority may be natural, but it seems misplaced. A man, who in the art gallery, spends his time discovering how the paintings were made, may well enjoy himself, may well be able to go away and make comparable pictures and should be in a good position to assess the achievements of the artist in his making process, but it is not clear that such a man will have stood back to respond to the pictures. There comes a point when you must stand back and attend to the rose madder flecked with cadmium yellow as the particular sky that it is. The situation seems comparable in the case of the musical theorist. If the Keller case is representative, then it seems fairly obvious that the analysis of what the music is made up of does not yield anything over and above knowledge of the music's constituents. It certainly does not follow that the music is uninteresting or bad because it remains in one key and is harmonically simple. We might be able to say of its composer that his ability to bring off unique and highly unlikely compositions at the level of musical theory was limited, without our having said anything about the quality of his work. We can say 'it is not musically very inventive' (meaning something like, it does not exercise to the full the repertoire of notes, keys, key changes, tempos, etc., open to the composer) 'not varied, rather repetitive, but it is the best piece of music I have ever heard'. The pop-dominated group with which Keller discussed music was not alarmed by the absence of key changes, or the presence of repetition.

It is not revealing and it is very obvious to say music is sound, but some grip must be kept on this fact in assessing the current theory. Musical notation has a logic of its own which can be explored independently of what it is a notation for. One could muse for hours on the possible permutations within musical theory without considering how these possibilities would sound. If one can read a score, the technical virtuosity of it may be apparent before one has read the score as music. Here then, we have echoes of the point made earlier in trying to locate the role of imagination in creation. One may well take delight in the purely formal qualities of a musical score, but this could have nothing to do with responding to the music. It is what happens when one listens to the sound, or what happens when the musical score one has understood in a purely logical way is brought to life in performance, that is important.

An analogy suggested above might be deemed weak. In the case of painting, or at least in the case of representational painting, one does have to stand back and see the pictorial whatever (sky, river, etc.), but the argument behind the musical theory view of music is that the same is not true of music. It is the case of music, it is alleged, that makes any representational theory of art invalid. It is granted that there is a form of music known as programme music, that there are operas, that films have background music, that there are ballets, but it is maintained that these areas, even if one could argue for them (and this is doubted) that their instances have specific references, are only some of the areas of music. As for the other areas the theory is that they must be quite unlike the case of representational painting. In response to this it must be conceded that if music could be held to represent, it could rarely represent as paintings do, or the idea of tying a piece of music down to a specific reference is absurd.

We now have two facts to be set alongside each other. Firstly, listening to music is listening to sound, and, thus, is not just a matter of attending to ingenious arrangements within musical notation at a purely formal level, and secondly, music cannot, without some absurdity, be tied down to acting as a specific representation, as is so in the case of painting. The second fact calls the earlier analogy into question whereas the first fact helps to redeem it.

The following seems to me to be some undeniable facts about listening to music.

The environment in which one listens can seem transformed by the music. The feeling is not that of being able to see the objects around one in a new way (e.g. in a more penetrating or truer fashion), as though the music increases one's powers of perception, but rather the music seems to layer over the objects of one's environment, transforming them in the process. It is just this characteristic of music which explains its use in films. One recognises this fact if one sees a film run through without background music and then with it. The addition of the music is not just the addition of another element like adding paper-money to a pile of coins; it is added as an active ingredient, working on the rest of the material. But, the room in which one sits listening to the music is the same room and is not altered by the presence of the music, it is only *as if* it is. The music runs a veneer over everything, but, of course, this is only a metaphor. It may be asked how things change, or appear to change, but to this there is unlikely to be any very precise answer. The change will vary from piece to piece, and even talk about a specific case will prove difficult. The fact remains that we recognise that such transformations occur. In a very general way only can we say, unobjectionably, what occurs. Things are made more dramatic, are intensified for us. In part, this occurs through the music appearing to give things expressive qualities that they do not possess. Further, as the use of music for dramatic purposes indicates, music is very flexible in suiting non-musical events. There are, of course, some pieces of music which cannot fir certain events, like trying to fit *June is Busting Out All Over* to Valentino's *The Four Horsemen of the Apocalypse*, but in the main one musical piece can have many separate uses. It is this fact which explains the inappropriateness of tying a piece of music down to a specific reference. This flexibility of the music allows one to use it to construct a drama out of the objects around one. The heavy bass notes apply to the big wooden table, the light notes on the flute one easily attaches to the vase on top, the relationship between these themes, in the music, invades the real relationship between vase and table. All of this enters into one's attention to the music without one having to make a special effort, on top of listening, to make it come about. Listening to the music is being drawn into the activity of making everything fit into it.

But some people insist on listening to music in the dark with their eyes shut. Is not this an attempt to reach the music as pure music? There are numerous responses to this. If it is thought this is what one is doing, then some implicit reference is made in this attempt to the way in which music tangles with the environment. Secondly, the darkness one plunges oneself into is something the music can take hold of and transform. Thirdly, with one's eyes shut the music has its maximum chance to act on one's imagination by stimulating mental imagery. And fourthly, the music itself invites its components to be seen as forces, events, beings, living out some life which the notations of musical theory will not describe. The bass notes will be turned into some unspecified force or presence which haunts or threatens or annihilates the lighter refrain. It is the aspect of music which is described accurately but generally in the recent theories of Morton Feldman and John Cage. Their conception of classical music is of something essentially theatrical, though the notion of theatre invoked is itself something slightly archaic. Classical music has a curtain and a proscenium arch and it lives out a drama. The audience is outside this world of the drama looking into it. Cage's experiments, however, lead him to make the listener part of the sound environment, in the sense that the listener's mode of existence will be, for some time at least, within it and that for part of the time the listener will be in control of that environment. There are similar developments in drama itself. The audience is invited into the drama to improvise and to propel it. What Cage produces is as much something falling under 'as if' descriptions as what his music is in reaction to. As in the case of drama proper, the development is one of the 'as if ' experience reaching out to embrace the audience not just to enable them to respond to the 'as if' experience in front of them, but so as to break down the barrier between audience and actor. Sometimes the destruction of this barrier is wrongly interpreted as breaking down the barrier between art and reality.

One thing which needs stressing and which certainly deserves greater exploration is the indefinite quality of the drama which music is. It is a drama without precisely specifiable characters and events (at the dramatic level, that is). The characters and events one can supply for oneself, although there will be some offers which are inappropriate, but the more important thing is that one can listen to it as drama without doing this. One listens to it as if there were precisely specifiable 'as if ' beings and events to witness, or rather it is that the music puts one into this attitude.

In addition to all of this we have the 'as if' implication of music's demands on our emotional resources. Listening to music is something we derive pleasure from. An evening spent listening to Tom Jones or Peter Pears is for the respective devotees an enjoyable experience likely to leave them satisfied and happy. This is the way in which music really works on our emotions. However, if one asks the question 'In what way does music work on our emotions?', one is unlikely to be referred to facts such as these, because the more important thing about music and our emotions seems to concern how we feel as we listen, and how the different passages in the music work upon us. But these reactions are not really emotional reactions, although it is *as if* they are. Normally, our reactions to the music are lightly dismissed. At the end of a Tom Jones' love song the woman may wipe away her tears breaking into applause and a beaming smile. Comparable reactions are as easily dismissed in listening to Bach. The sadness the music engenders is not real sadness, because if it was it would make no sense to explain the audience's continuing presence at the performance as something due to the enjoyment they gained from the music. This point applies to the range of emotions that come into our talk about our reactions to music. The emotional commitment is not real because the alleged emotions do not have real objects. Moreover, they do not involve appropriate behaviour (e.g. the fear which seems to possess us in listening to some eerie passage in the music does not lead to our removing ourselves from the presence of the music) and, further, they are fickle, coming and going with the rise and fall of the music. What fits the nature of the experience are images of emotion, thus, we enter into 'as if' emotional states. Apart from objections stemming from a lack of detail in the account I have just put forward, there seem to me to be two objections that might be made. Firstly, it might be objected that such an account is a serious reduction of the response we make to music. The experiences we derive from music we regard, or are regarded, as large and important, and yet on the present account they become a number of 'as if' experiences. However, this is only a reduction of significant experiences if we underrate the significance of the 'as if'. It is my purpose to stress the overwhelming nature of the 'as if', and the way in which it appears to provide us with our richest and most intense experiences. Secondly, there might be the objection that I have been describing the experience of the average concert-goer, the kind of person who can listen to a recital of Bach organ music and yet tell jokes going home afterwards. The suggestion might be that I should have taken as a paradigm the person who is most deeply impressed by the music, people like composers themselves, persons who go home after the concert with the music continuing to haunt them. However, to have taken this case would not have been to point unambiguously to real emotional involvement with music, for it could as well be argued that here was a case of someone who cannot, or will not, shut off 'as if' experiences; a person dominated by a life in the sphere of the 'as if'. Composers are such people.

In conclusion, I have argued against what I have been calling the musical theory view of music, and argued for an understanding of music as involving the 'as if', and have done this by (a) trying to explain the impulse towards the former theory as stemming from some misunderstanding of what the latter theory involves, and (b) by arguing positively for the latter theory.

10

Attacking correspondence as a defence of art and determining the criteria for convincingness

The primary demand we make of 'entertainment objects' is convincingness. This is to say we demand of them 'magnetic as if features' which are experienced as gripping or real.

There are theories which make convincingness depend upon correspondence. Such theories provide arguments for the superiority of art. Any account displacing a correspondence theory, and which advances the thesis of my earlier book (*Art an Enemy of the People*), will have to make clear the idea that the differing mental sets of the classes in bourgeois society make some convincing things appear unconvincing to sections of this kind of society. This need is based on the premise that convincingness is objectively determinable. This is a premise that will need a little attention.

In his article 'Art and Reality'[53] Hospers is attributed with a correspondence theory of convincingness. For instance, Danto in his article, 'Imagination, Reality and Art', so interprets Hospers.[54] However, a careful inspection of what is not an over-precise article (nor an article intended as such) shows one can accept its main argument without holding a correspondence theory. When it is seen how this is possible it becomes clear that Hosper's tells us little about convincingness. On the surface, there is a correspondence theory right enough. Thus, we are told, for a character to be convincing it must be true to human nature. However, if we probe, we find the notion of human nature to which characters must conform is not given through a collection of empirical sightings. Therefore, Danto is not altogether relevant in arguing that with Hosper's account the plausibility or convincingness of a character could depend upon pointing to a person like the character (person and character thus giving substance to a character-type). This for Hospers would be an exceedingly oblique way of indicating plausibility. His thesis is much more that our concept of human nature imposes logical restrictions on what is to count as a person. Thus, we are told, if an author has built up a character as one seriously facing a problem, he cannot retain plausibility if the character suddenly and flippantly, without any preparation on the author's part, gives up the problem. Hospers is not saying volatile and mercurial personalities cannot be rendered plausible in literature, rather he is pointing to logical limitations. The thesis is that where the developments of the novel abuse the criteria of personal identity, then we can no longer believe in the identity of a character who has so developed. This seems fairly reasonable, for accepting someone as a persisting human being should be dependent upon the specimen meeting some conditions. Therefore, I take Hospers as saying that a convincing character must conform to our concept of human nature. 'Character' is a word we would apply to Piglet and Pooh, but for Hospers this is only so because they are personifications. I doubt the word is so restricted, but if it is it does not seem rash to tie it to what the concept of human nature will allow as human nature. However, this tie tells us a minimal amount about the convincingness of characters. To write,

He lived in Leeds before moving to London. When he got to London he married his first wife and they went to Gibraltar for their honeymoon, where he got drunk quite a lot and discovered his true homosexual nature ...

is to begin a narrative that in no way exceeds the concept of human nature as might,

She was a lovely girl even while she was himself and he did have a lovely time never allowing herself to finish a thought, both in Paris and Berlin at the same time. Goodness, he did enjoy being intensely depressed, I have never seen anyone so spry and alive in an exuberant fit of despair.

If the possibility of the first sample is contained within the concept of a person and the possibility of the second sample not, it does not follow that the man of the first sample is a convincing character. This is not because the first sample is too short; it is not hard to imagine extending the passage in similar fashion so as to be left with an account of a man's life (fictional or otherwise) but not to be left with a convincing character. For a character to be convincing it must be more than possible, it must also be real. The reality of a character is so separate a thing from the character's possibility that we may feel a sense of reality about a proffered character without knowing about the logical possibility of such a person. The second sample might seem to make someone (no one) come alive, whereas the definite someone of the first sample remains obstinately leaden.

A clearer example of a correspondence theorist is M.H. Abrams in his essay 'Belief and the Suspension of Disbelief'.[55] Though at the outset Abrams takes up Bradley's famour view as being basically correct, namely, that the validity of a work depends upon its parts cohering, and not on an overall correspondence between it and the world, eventually he tries a synthesis of the two views by maintaining that successful coherence depends ultimately on successful correspondence. One of his concluding remarks is: 'There is no escaping the circumstances that a poet must submit to the conditions of human nature in order to be their master.' It is not altogether clear what this means, and it would be possible to construe it as Hospers's thesis has been, but the tenor of Abrams's discussion makes it clear that correspondence to the actual conditions of human life is what he has in mind, and not the compatibility with the concept of human nature (or the concept of a person). He constantly reiterates that where a work of literature embodies a moral attitude (and that it does may for Abrams be a necessary feature of it), then the moral attitude must conform with the reader's moral attitudes if the reader is to allow the work a sense of reality and thus allow it to take a grip on his mind. The sense of reality is identified as the coherence of the work and its criterion is correspondence. That this is Abrams's view is brought out by quotations, thus, 'All these results, however distinguishable from our responses in practical life, depend in great part on beliefs and dispositions which we bring to the poem from life'; and 'But King Lear presents a conflict of characters in which the author must make us take sides; and he is able to do so only by presupposing that we bring to the work deep-rooted moral beliefs and values which will cause us instinctively to attach our good will to some characters and ill will to others . . . .'

In *Literature and Belief,* Cleanth Brooks produces a more muddled (as it seems to me) version of the same thesis in his article 'Implications of an Organic Theory of Poetry'.[56] He writes,

For the coherence of parts in a literary work depends upon our belief in the plausibility of certain human actions and reactions, responses and valuations . . . . That such a picture of human nature has definite implications for nature in general—for reality itself—I should be the first to acknowledge . . . .

The sins committed by the artist . . . are best described as violations of coherence: the exploitation of the sentimental, of the merely sensational, of the monstrous and in general all obfuscations of human perception and action.

In accordance with this theory Brooks finds Antigone 'deeply and admirably human' though Greek burial rites are not ours, but finds Williams's Serafina delle Rosa impossible to believe in, even though she may be sociologically sound. Serafina delle Rosa seems to fail as a credible human being because though she may correspond, she corresponds with what is depraved; the indictment (hardly made clear by Brooks) seems to be that the playwright's outlook is depraved. Despite Tennessee Williams's failure, it is for Brooks a dictum of poetry 'that poetry is a kind of reality refracted through subjective responses'.

For both these critics, then, a work's convincingness depends upon its internal order, yet the requisite internal order requires correspondence. If we enquire as to what kind of factors the correspondence is to consist in, it seems the work must present persons and human situations as they are, and in so doing must yield a moral assessment of these persons and their situations with which we concord (our agreement only being possible because we have morally assessed actual persons and situations in a similar way, or are already committed to morally assessing in this way). It is allowed we may not share the particular creed the writer adopts, but the view seems to be that our particular moral preoccupations have a substratum of more general moral attitudes, and it is these we must hold in common if the work is to be found plausible.

Whether or not a work of literature can be attributed with a moral view is, I think, more difficult to decide than is often allowed (a didactic poem perhaps can, a play perhaps cannot), but waiving this, if the work says (to take the easiest case) character A is a good man and B bad, then even if the work is inconvincing unless we agree with this, it does not follow that some moral belief we *took* to the work now has something to apply to. The world created by the work may be for us something unique, and it may be the moral belief we take up in response to it is new to us. I can see no justification for Abrams's claim that the attachment of our goodwill to some characters in a work stems from deep-rooted moral beliefs that we bring to the work from life. It could be that the work brings about a total moral conversion in ourselves, or constitutes our initiation into moral education. On the other hand, it could engage our moral sense as it is not engaged in any other context. It would seem, then, that if a work expresses a moral attitude about its action, then the most we can say, in concurring with this attitude, is that if there were situations of this kind then we would bring this attitude to them; we do not have to say 'this is a moral belief I have held all along'.

We are back with the position that characterises Hospers's account, namely, the convincingness of a work is dependent upon it giving us a possible world and possible views of that world. To maintain this is to hold to much less than the correspondence theorist holds, yet even holding this much is not without its problems.

In F. Kermode's *The Sense of an Ending*[57] an argument using the views of Sartre and Iris Murdoch is put forward to suggest that characters are necessarily fictions. This is not meant in the obvious sense that in fiction they will be fictional, but in the sense that no *such* persons *could* exist. The problems is one posed by existentialism. The argument is that if a man is free, his kind cannot exist in novels as the lives of characters are determined, for, if this was not the case we could not sustain an interest in them. Proponents of this line of argument would not accept what I claimed was really Hospers's interpretation of the man who suddenly jumps out of character; for them, he may be unconvincing as a character in a novel, but need not be any abuse of personal identity criteria. The argument is that the writer makes puppets and not men, and his problem, whether he realises it or not, is to appear to give them autonomy of will (or often this is the problem), and this has to be done without allowing them to disrupt the necessary determining structure of the novel. For Iris Murdoch this is very much *the* problem for the novelist; the problem of how to make your creations appear to have free will when they cannot have it.

If the world of the novel necessarily gives us a reality of determined beings, then, of course, this does not conflict with the requirement that it must give a possible world: the determinist's case is at least plausible. But if the position the correspondence theorist is to be reduced to is that of convincingness being dependent on the work providing a possible *human* reality, then this is in conflict with the considerations just brought forward, if, that is, being human means being free.

Without investigating the existentialist view of freedom it is possible to take an indeterminist position, and to allow that some of the concepts, important to the understanding of characters in novels, are incompatable with indeterminism being true of those characters. Such concepts are ones like 'destiny', 'fate', 'law of x's nature'. In fact, one view of tragedy is that of a person (because of internal and external constraints and complusions) performing the inevitable. The characters for whom such concepts are required are not necessarily unconvincing, in fact they may be the most compelling and real. Unless we should maintain real persons have destinies (where 'destiny' is employed in a full-blooded sense) we have to admit that the convincingness of literary characters is not dependent upon correspondence to the paradigms of human existence. So we may have correspondence, or just the appearance of correspondence (e.g. appearing free but not being so), or, no correspondence at all, just bare possibility, and, perhaps, we can have the case of total impossibility without it being a clear case of total unconvincingness. An interesting comparison here is the case of M. C. Escher's lithographs where impossible perspectives give the appearance of possibility.

It is against a background of trying to explain convincingness through correspondence that the critic thinks he finds a way of demonstrating the superiority of art over the rest of those things being referred to as 'entertainment objects'. The critic is also tempted to think that some version of a correspondence theory enables him to demonstrate that in a general way the arts are about the same kind of thing as other 'noble' human pursuits, namely, the acquisition of truth in some shape of form.

It is my contention that because of the strong sense of reality transmitted or carried by works one accepts, there is a temptation to account for the sense of reality through some correspondence theory ('it seems so real; things must be thus'). The tempted critic has to find a satisfactory correspondence theory. Notoriously the critic finishes up with something so vague (e.g. some very non-committal account of what is to pass as truth) that one feels it makes no difference whether one has it or not. Alternatively, the philosopher, with similar inclinations, takes on the same problem and though proposing a clearer theory, produces something ultimately irrelevant, as does Hospers in *Meaning and Truth in the Arts*,[58] where the 'truth to/truth about' distinction reduces to what the concept of human nature allows and what empirical propositions about men specify. Some of the links proposed between art and reality will be looked into later when various challenges to the present line of argument are entertained, but for the moment what is required is an account of convincingness which is not a correspondence theory.

In summary form the reasons for not expecting explanations from correspondence theories are:

(1)   The unsatisfactory character of existing theories.

(2)   The way in which they all seem to reduce to some claim about compatibility with possibilities, which preempts them of any significance as correspondence theories.

(3)   The fact that there are reasons for seeing much of literature as being about a form of life clearly not human.

In addition to this can be added the fact that convincingness of the work is something judged, though the audience knows it is in no position to judge correspondence. We do not have to wait on experience to judge a works convincingness, correspond or not, and whether we know it corresponds or not, we are in a position to assess the works convincingness.

On what then does the convincingness of a work depend? It seems to me the answer is that for the works which are convincing we need to tell a different story in each case. What makes the novels of Tolstoy convincing will differ from what makes the novels of Dostoevsky convincing. If for a moment we think of Tolstoy and Dostoevsky as conjurors or magicians we may say the convincingness of their tricks depends upon their respective techniques. It is not that what they do corresponds with how things are, or how things proceed normally, for tricks are not made of such stuff, but it is in their art, their own brands of wizardry, that they bring us to accept as vivid, as if they were real, a range of abnormal happenings. To explain the convincingness of *War and Peace* will be to exhibit much of Tolstoy's artistry (i.e. the way in which he makes the 'as if' real). The explanation required has nothing to do with checking *War and Peace* against Russian history, or its characters against our range of acquaintances.

These remarks can be generalised. Thus, 'entertainment objects' are convincing when their 'as if' features are strongly 'as iffy', and this is achieved by producing something strongly like or strongly as if it were a state of affairs other than it is. The state of affairs it is to be like need not be actual. One makes the 'entertainment object' convincing by making it strongly as if it were what it is meant to be like. The problem, for the maker, is to make something (to use a 'hippy' phrase) 'like real', rather than to make something like what is real (already). The required sense of reality is conveyed in the case where something is made like what is real, only if it is an instance of the other thing described (i.e. being like real). The maker of successful 'entertainment objects' has the capacity to give his works this strong sense of reality. To understand what this involves we have to investigate the particular techniques employed. At a philosophical level all we need understand is that the problem of making something seem real is not the problem of making something seem like something, or a kind of something, which *is* real. The creation of, the nature of and the response to the 'as if ' make perfectly good sense without tying it down to what is already real.

It was said at the outset of this chapter that the primary demand made of 'entertainment objects' is that they be convincing. To judge the object as convincing is to acclaim it as satisfacory, but it is to do more than this. The term 'convincing' denotes the degree of reality attained by the 'as iffy' features of a work. This quality of convincingness seems both universal and indispensible. This is harldy surprising if it is indeed an important feature of the collection of things being considered that they have 'as if' characteristics. Consider the range covered in the following list of questions: Is Nicolai Gedda convincingly Don José. Is Hamlet a convincing character? Was Pavlova a convincing swan? Is Vermeer's *A Lady Reading a Letter* a convincing space? Are Moore's sculptures convincingly part of a landscape? Are Salvador Dali's paintings convincingly atmospheric? Is King Kong a convincing monster? Does the world of Simon Templar convince? Is *She's Leaving Home* convincingly sad? does Sinatra do a convincing *Old Man River*? This list of questions shows some of the ways in which convincingness matters. However, simple questions like these fail to get at the convincingness of certain experiences of 'entertainment objects'. Thus, in listening to a Janacek string quartet, or in following *The Desert Song* or *Hair,* one quickly moves through a series of 'as if' states which in retrospect get organised into a satisfying whole, and about which it would be difficult to ask if the works mentioned convincingly conveyed the whole of that experience, i.e. there would be some difficulty in giving a specific enough description of that whole experience.

So the argument to date is this: there is a feature general enough for us to say it is sought in all experiences of art. This feature is a necessary feature of art and is what is important about art, yet it is not a defining feature of art. It is a feature possessed by many other things that do not fall under the heading of art. The class of things possessing this feature are being referred to as 'entertainment objects', and the feature they possess, or aim at possessing, will be that of being convincingly 'as iffy'. The possession of this feature is not dependent upon correspondence.

The next stage of the argument requires space to be made for two different points. One point is that mental sets (like the mental set which may go with a certain class position in society) upset, or make possible, the perception of convincingness in 'entertainment objects'. The other point is that judgments about convincingness are corrigible. Ultimately, therefore, what has to be done is to distinguish between two kinds of dispute. One of which, to all appearance, is based on a difference of taste, the other of which shows that one of the positions in the other dispute *can* be supported, and is not just a matter of taste.

This needs to be done for two reasons. Firstly, it is my thesis that there is no qualitative distinction to be drawn between high and low culture 'entertainment objects', and that the distinction so often drawn is bogus. Secondly, I wish to recognise the fact that unsuccessful 'entertainment objects' are produced. As regards the first reason it should be clear why I think a bogus distinction is often drawn (the influence of social class), and further the denial of a qualitative distinction does indeed mean that I hold *The Sound of Music* to be on a par with *Aida*, or whichever other cross-cultural examples might seem appropriate. As regards the second reason, what I have in mind are obvious facts like not all pop songs being equally good, or not all of Beethoven's symphonies being as good as each other. The thesis to be supported, then, is that class differences explain the way in which distinctions are made between, say, classical and pop music. In the case of music, it is a significant piece of evidence, in favour of this thesis, that where the upper-middle class begins to concern itself with pop it is there that a discussion begins about the place of pop in art. It really does seem to be the case that if it is entertainment by means of the 'as if ', and if it is covered consistently by, say, *The Observer* or *The Sunday Times* then *ipso facto* it is art.

To make the first of the two points mentioned let me draw attention to some very ordinary facts about our responses to 'entertainment objects'. It must be a well-known fact that the working-class audience finds it very difficult to be interested in Shakespeare or Ionesco or Brecht, etc. It is tempting to say this is because much of it goes over their heads, or because (as in the Shakespeare case) they have difficulty with the language. The point made is that with the right kind of education

these experiences become open to them, without it, ignorance
defeats them. It is certain that with the right kind of education
these experiences do become open to them, but it is highly
debatable that education is something neutral here. Succeeding in the educational system involves either reinforcing one's
middle-class position, or becoming middle class. Education is
a passport to middle-class life. With education, therefore, one
takes on the outlook which makes Shakespeare, Ionesco and
Brecht acceptable. The major difficulty the working-class
audience has with high culture 'entertainment objects' is one
of style or format. For this audience the style or the format of
the piece works against its convincingness, or rather though
the work is convincing its style prevents this particular
audience from finding it so. For instance, long speeches are
things whose ends the working-class audience looks forward
to, they are things to be got through, and if anything is
interesting it is what one may find either end of them. The
objection to the long speech is that it is not natural, yet to
someone engrossed in the play the speech is accepted as
something perfectly natural. 'Naturalness' is just another way
of talking about convincingness. A working-class complaint
about Shakespeare concerns its unconvincing flow of time;
the plays are found too slow. Yet to the adherent the plays
have an electrifying and gripping pace. On the other hand the
working-class complaint about Brecht, in a play like *The
Threepennny Opera*, might be that it moves too quickly, that
it does not give itself time to develop what it has got. What to
the adherent is a canvas flashing with a myriad of detail is to
the working-class too diffuse and bitty to be interesting. What
I am talking about are not things which out-strip the intelligence of the class which objects to them, for I am referring to
things which are matters of convention. An acceptance of the
conventions is the barrier, and it is clear that which conventions you can accept depends upon which conventions you
have been favourably exposed to. The working-class is exposed to high-cultural objects in school but, given the mental
set of the class, this cannot count as favourable exposure.

   That conventions can be the big stumbling block is evidenced in the area of high culture, where often the new
conventions of a new work account for its failure with its

public. This situation works the other way round. There are works where the conventions for the working-class audience are acceptable. Where for this class there is a gripping authentic drama there is for the high-cultural audience something totally unconvincing and laughable. Scorn is what the working-class itself brings to high cultural 'entertainment objects', where great expressive moments of grief or joy seem to them laughably unreal. Of course, the objection is likely to be that *The Sound of Music* is laughably unreal, is totally unconvincing, and that *Aida* is a very real and convincing work, but this is too simple. The argument used to demonstrate the unconvincingness of *The Sound of Music* sooner or later deteriorates into an argument about its lack of correspondence, but a lack of correspondence does not bear directly on the reality of a work. Moreover, the demand for correspondence cannot be met honestly by more than a few high-cultural 'entertainment objects'. Further, it is a conspicuous fact about some recent members of the intelligentsia, who stem from working-class stock, that their attitude towards high and low cultural 'entertainment objects' is somewhat ambiguous. David Mercer's Morgan might symbolise the type. He is a person who can just make out in a high cultural setting (his difficulty is emotional and has little to do with an inability to assimilate the conventions) yet he is enthralled by 'Tarzan' films. For Morgan the experience of 'Tarzan' is not simply the fashionable thing to do, it is an utterly gripping and real experience. The reaction of the intelligentsia at National Film Theatres though benign has nothing to do with Morgan's raptures over Tarzan's escapades. If the high-cultural objects were really the convincing ones, and low-cultural objects were unconvincing, it ought to be the case that coming to appreciate high-cultural objects, through a successful education, would reveal the unconvincingness of objects that once seemed so very real. Perhaps the teacher feels that his job is splendidly done if he brings the student to such a set of beliefs. Undoubtably, this kind of conversion often occurs, and this is not so surprising seeing that success in literary studies at a fairly high level requires the techniques and beliefs which commit one to scathing reviews of productions like *The Sound of Music*. It seems almost unthinkable that a strict academic success in literary studies (say the man who takes a First at a university) could be well disposed towards *The Sound of Music*. Certainly it is more often the person who cannot quite submit to the regimentation which makes for a strict academic success who finds himself with a penchant for low-cultural objects. It is extremely unlikely that someone with a strong upper-middle-class background will ever be in the same position, although it can become fashionable and has to concern oneself with low-cultural objects. The point is, however, that the appreciation of both kinds of objects is possible without either response being really any different from the normal response these objects draw to themselves. On the objection that appreciation of the one must undermine appreciation of the other such cases could not occur, but clearly they do.

The upshot of the view that both high and low-cultural objects can be convincing, or give rise to convincing experiences, and that things seem otherwise because of the mental sets we develop, must be a plea for greater tolerance. To put it in its strongest form an attack on *The Sound of Music* is an attack on working-class taste and as soon as we see it in this form it becomes clearly intolerable. If reviews of things like *The Sound of Music* are necessary, then the authentic voice is the one for which the piece works. One would be able to tell from this whether or not one could accept the conventions of the work. The working-class *does* make fun of Shakespeare; although its views are denied the permanence of the printed article. There is nothing admirable in this, for the truth is that different kinds of objects work for different social classes, and similarly, different kinds of objects work for different kinds of societies (e.g. certain forms of primitive 'art', as we now call it, could not have been accepted by the high bourgeosie of certain periods and places). None of this is meant as recommendation to open ourselves to as many of the conventions as possible, for sufficient 'entertainment objects' are enough. There are things to be said for reading nothing but Henry James and things against reading anything and everything.

To turn now to the other point mentioned — the question of corrigibility. In general, we may say judgments about convincingness are not incorrigible, because it is possible that the conventions have been inexpertly handled, or rather that we can see through their use to the person who is using them. So really we have a distinction between different kinds of things, all of which can possess convincingness, and things of a kind which may be more or less successful at possessing the same feature. To take an example, Longfellow's *Hiawatha* is not altogether an unconvincing work, but it fails to bite home as real. Now one explanation of this might be that it paints an untrue picture of Indian life, that Longfellow sees the Indian through European blinkers, and that his anthropology is very weak. This explanation would point to a lack of correspondence between the poem and the fact. This line of explanation has to be distinguished from another, where we say that Longfellow tries to give his poem the mood and atmosphere of an alien culture, but that what we detect is the usual atmosphere and world, plus a sighting of the poet trying to graft on atmospheric titbits that we detect too easily as not belonging. The correspondence explanation really is irrelevant, for though the poem might be untrue of Indian life it is possible that it could create a fresh and convincing world which would be absorbing. If it tries to confront the reader with a fresh world, the trouble lies in our being able to see that this is what Longfellow is about. We see him trying; we do not witness his success. This kind of failure is possible in any area of 'entertainment objects'; it is, to revert to an earlier analogy, the failure of the magician to conceal how he does it.

Now, just as it is possible for someone to find Longfellow's poem utterly convincing and be wrong about this (like the child who is not watchful enough to see the magician has bungled the trick) so it is possible for someone to think the work is unconvincing because its maker's hand shows too clearly, when, in fact, his finding it unconvincing is a matter of his not being able to respond to the conventions. It may not be easy always to tell whether it is the maker's inefficiency or the audience's inability to take on the conventions, and careful investigation may be required to make the distinction.

Convincingness, then, is both a property of something and something in the eye of the beholder. It is important (for reasons given and reasons as yet not given) and it is something not confined to art.

11

The nature of the attraction of the 'as if'

The arguments of the last chapter entail that 'entertainment objects' can satisfy us in conveying a strong sense of an independent world. On the other hand the world conveyed may not be independent, but what will be important about it will be how *like real* it is, and not the extent to which it is true of the world on which it depends. In a rather special sense of independent, therefore, we can say 'entertainment objects' satisfy through their presentation of an independent world. The presented world, resembling reality or not, is independent in that it has to be strongly *as if* that world is present. To this extent it is like the peep-show. The peep-show may be of the room we inhabit, but, despite the reference, it is independent of it, in the sense that it has the brightness and immediacy of appearing to be there. Having *the being there* of what we say it is like, is the nature of the appropriate likeness involved. This is a feature of magnetic 'as if' situations. The idea of a world, and of a peep-show for that matter, is too confined. They suggest too much an 'as iffy' object, apart from ourselves, to which we give attention, whereas, often, the 'entertainment object' is not so much a peep-show as an hallucinatory drug (this is only an analogy), which is to say it generates 'as if' experiences and states without being a magnetic 'as if' object in itself (the 'tactilator' in the first chapter is an extreme example of this). However, I shall continue to refer to 'independent worlds' using the term to cover a range of phenomena.

If we derive satisfaction from entering into these independent worlds, as presented to us by 'entertainment objects', the question arises as to how this is. What is the basis of our attraction to independent worlds presented in this way?

Thinking about independent worlds more generally, it seems true that the 1960s more than any other recent decade saw an upsurge of belief in the value of independent worlds. Sub-cultures, the Underground, experiments with drugs all included affirmations of this interest. This interest did not go unmixed with belief that independent worlds constituted a way to truth. This aspect of these trends made them absurd. Thus, it was claimed ultimate reality is perceived through the use of LSD, or that really the independent world is the world of the mind and that a journey into it is justified as an exploration of the mind. In similar fashion various experiences of an 'as iffy' character were regarded as having transcendental or religious significance. Just as absurdly the world of the schizophrenic was seen as being of heroic proportions. The schizophrenic, instead of being seen as a shattered person, was seen as a traveller in an unknown region, capable of bringing back insights into some of the most primitive forces that move us. 'Schizophrenic' became something to be, something to aim at, something noble. In terms of trends, then, various things were bracketed together, including belief in independent worlds, drug experience, being mad, and as an integral part of this whole scene 'entertainment objects', especially pop and what (or some of what) is art.

Despite the absurdities the good thing about this movement was its unapologetic affirmation of engrossment in independent worlds. This might be seen as the seeking of fantasy, but this is to misdescribe what is sought. A fantasy world is merely a sub-class of independent worlds, to be distinguished by means of the simple structure of its world, as well as by the bizarre way in which it departs from the world inhabited by its audience. A sizeable minority of a generation, therefore deliberately courted independent worlds, and more than this thought it possible to live totally engrossed in independent worlds. What was envisaged was much more than the normal intrusion of art into the life of the high bourgeoisie. Possibly, therefore, it is appropriate in the immediate post-hippy period that reflective activity should concern itself with our participation in the unreal. To reiterate the earlier question then, '*what* constitutes the basis of our interest in independent worlds?'

The relevant situations are magnetic 'as if' situations which are recognised as such. They are taken on as 'as if' situations. If we are in trouble it is difficult to be captivated by the 'as ifness' of a situation. For instance, a man who awaits execution, and minds about it, is unlikely to be able to watch his favourite programme *Coronation Street* and find it as convincing and gripping as usual on the eve of execution. Perhaps, if he is very fatalistic or resigned, he might, but not otherwise. An even better case might be that of a man who is very hungry. But these are cases in which the hurt is not derived from the 'as if' situation itself. Consider though this possibility. A sultry maiden in chainmail bikini lays one on a couch in a vineyard and proceeds to brush one lightly with what appears to be a feather. Other temptations abundantly surround one. However, what appears to be a feather, what is only 'as if' it is a feather, is a razor-sharp sword. Further, one has been told one is condemned to death and one knows this is inevitable. One is to be beheaded with a quick flash of the feather-like sword. To what extent, or can one to any extent, regard this state of affairs as being strongly 'as if' one has fallen into a harem and is to be seduced? Surely, one could not detach oneself from one's plight to think 'how real this is, how convincing'. If one had time to think one might say this situation is like seduction within the harem. However, it is not as though the situation forces the thought of the execution being the seduction. One is unable to respond to the situation as a magnetic 'as if' situation. Ulysses's crew, it may be remembered, were taken prisoner by Circe. Her device, it seems, was to trap them through drugs in a world of dreams. They stay willingly, though their real purpose is to return. However, the prison of dreams can only work in so far as it is not recognised (a) as being dreams and (b) as having obliterated the original purpose. Without the obliteration we would have to see Ulysses's crew as not regarding the unfulfilment of the original purpose as of so great a consequence: under those circumstances it might not count as a penalty, as later it does not for Ulysses. Given the penalty is so severe the feather-like, titillator-like object would be seen as the instrument of destruction. Similarly, the seductress would lose this aspect in the eye of the victim, and become for him what she is, the executioner. But what of the masochist who derives sexual satisfaction from his masochistic experiences, would he not court the 'as if' interpretation of the events despite the penalty? The masochist would open himself to both aspects of the situation. He would respond to the sexual connotations and also to the threatening finale of the charade. If he perceives the situation in 'as if' terms (and this itself is not altogether clear for what at the 'as if' level is a sexual illusion becomes for him a real sexual experience) it is only because the reality of the situation is not something he truly minds about. The 'as if' dissolves as we find the situation decreasingly innocuous. A phenomenon which images this point is the smile of the torturor. To the victim, or even to the onlooker, he cannot be seen as giving a convincing impression of friendliness: as we mind so much about what he is really doing this aspect of his conduct invades his dissembling.

Thus, our concern with independent worlds involves us in becoming convincingly part of an experience which is necessarily harmless. With independent worlds we get the feel of ranging through experiences without really doing so. But why should this be attractive? At present we have a very incomplete answer.

The experiences are not only viewed by the recipient as being without danger but as being richer, and more complete or shaped or purposeful than his experience of reality. In this there is a hint as to how the harmless, penaltyless character of the 'as if' is to be understood. The 'as if' experiences one ranges through do not just remove the possibility of obvious harms like physical pain or death. These are the easiest and most straightforward cases to use as examples, but they hardly do justice to the complexity of the field. Take the case of a play which convincingly conveys a certain love affair. Why should one concern oneself with this? Does it have some attraction stemming from its 'as if' form? Would not some first-hand experience of a love affair be more satisfying than the experience of this 'as if' situation could ever be? This is really the Fogle-Richards objection to Hulme (examined in Chapter 5). However, a love affair lived through is never up to a love affair fictionalised, or if at moments it seems to be this is because we make the real into a fiction. The fictionalised love affair forces us to focus in a certain way, it gives us nothing but emphasis, it simplifies and makes out the simplification is all there is, it is a one-dimensional world, whereas the world we inhabit is infinitely dimensional. The real love affair contains among other things, the dirt between the toes, the thoughtless moments on the lavatory, bad breath and sanitary towels. This is not to say 'entertainment objects' do not deal with grime for we know the contrary to hold, the point is the actual world is without meaning, whereas independent worlds are not. Even if we believe the world is meaningful, or that our lives have meaning, or that the circumstances we live through have a shape, it seems clear that the interwoven character of the independent world gives a more perfect whole, an exaggerated sense of completeness. It contains fewer loose threads, and so protects us from the necessary penalty of reality.

It is likely to be argued that a sense of wholeness or completeness is very much a genre of 'entertainment objects', that it is a convention and one which is at present being questioned.[59] The suggestion is likely to be that the idea of the world as formless and meaningless is very much a modern phenomenon, and one very much attributable to existentialism. Artists have responded to this idea, they have tried to make films, paintings, novels, etc., which convey the formlessness of experience. It might be contended that such a movement is responsible for the demise of story and plot in many contemporary works of art. '(This discussion is confined to the category of art, for it is only here that the problem has been raised.) However, a distinction is required. A film may be an assemblage of fragments, and may lack continuity in the traditional sense, but, despite this, it may try to give a glimpse of the totality. In many cases this glimpse is meant as something rare, as something especially provided by the film, which is to say it is not a view given in the experience of reality, though this experience may give grounds for judging the film's correspondence. There is a difference between a juxtaposition of fragments giving a glimpse of a totality, and living through the fragments. This is a difference of viewpoint, it is the difference between experiencing something as complete and total, and not being able to do so. Further, quite apart from the intentions of the film maker the fact one is watching film imposes a global viewpoint. One's position is the spectator's, and the fact that one spectates film confines one in this role. One cannot enter the world of the film as agent. The spectator's view, whether the object viewed is in an 'as iffy' medium or not, is essentially global and complete. Of course, the perception of totality can be a matter of degree, for the totality perceived can be of greater or lesser organisation. The spectator's role alone guarantees the minimal global perception. Thus, a film not aiming at giving a fast glimpse of the totality through a juxtaposition of fragments, but which gave many fragments in something approaching the order and temporal sequence of succeeding phases of reality, would provide us with no greater a totality than what we derive from being spectators. The experience of such a film would likely to be tedious. Such films are made and it seems tedium is the common experience associated with them.

The present argument is advanced without clinging to the idea of the meaninglessness of life; the argument does not depend on the solidity of a certain theme in existentialist thinking. The 'entertainment object' conveys a greater sense of significance and meaning, an exaggerated pattern, and beginning and end are necessarily of significance and cannot be totally arbitrary points. Perhaps examples can be thought of which do not appear to conform to this ruling, but then arbitrarily chosen beginnings and ends are exhibited against a background of beliefs concerning the sameness of the things depicted and the things not depicted. In which case the beginnings and ends take on significance, for they encapsulate the essentials of the subject. In the cinema there are moments when the end seems to depend upon no more than the camera running out of film. This is as much a matter of choice and artifice as is fading out on a glorious sunset. The point of the device is to say, 'this is how it is, there are no grand moments in an operatic sense, we end simply because the film runs out'. We are left with the thought that life will go on similarly and that we have stopped looking at it and that is all. However, the film forces us into a comprehensive outlook, we are directed to a summation. The outlook in life is otherwise, for ordinarily we move on and that is all. Of course, there are moments when we need summations (even if these summations are themselves fictions) but, in the case of the film the comprehensive outlook is a necessary attitude, we cannot just move on. A difference, then, between the world and independent worlds is that the former lacks meaning as compared with the latter. It is in this sense that we must understand how the independent world keeps us from the penalties of the world. Of course, in the world we can seek out the comprehensive attitude. The leisure of the bourgeois aesthete has been built around this purpose. To command a view of some bay and the Mediterranean from a good elevation in the Appenines is to be in comprehensive mood, but the mood is undermined by its passing, for one's experience continues to be of the same world though one's perception of it becomes bitty. However, after the experience of the 'entertainment object' the subsequent bitty perceptions, which come on one in the street having left the cinema, or having put down the book and gone walking, involve one in the feeling that one has switched from one world to another. There is a sense of two dimensions; it is with differing experiences of one dimension that the experiences undermine each other.

In distinguishing between man and animals perhaps the truth is that nothing in the life of man is as it is in the life of the animal. However, if we are looking for the most prominent differences we should have to point to man's creative capacities. This difference is often cited, and is often followed by a list of examples taken from high bourgeois culture, for instance the Sistine ceiling or the Appollo Belevedere. Something more banal is intended in this context, however. Man's ability to hold a possibility before the mind is all that is really meant. Maybe animals can be credited with this ability, but then the distinction depends upon the degree to which the ability is exercised. As much in an ordinary as in an allegedly extraordinary man the degree to which the ability is exercised is pronounced as compared with animals. We might say an animal is thinking of its next meal (i.e. thinking of a possibility) when it desplays meal-expectant behaviour (though it is unclear what we mean by this assertion), but except in most unusual circumstances an animal is not said to hatch plans, whereas a man can hardly live as a man without doing so. The exercise of this ability can be divided into two fairly distinct enterprises. Firstly, there is its use where it is demanded by man's situation, where it is we might say materially necessary. Secondly, there is its more gratuitous use, where its exercise is very much in free play. 'Entertainment objects' are often the result of the second use, although there are many specific cases of them being materially necessitated. Marx held, in *German Ideology*, that division of labour gave rise to the division of material and mental activity, and from this division consciousness layed claim to being a world unto itself. Whether or not this possibility for human consciousness arose as Marx suggests is irrelevant. What is of importance in this context is that this does seem a very special feature of the human condition. We have man's consciousness necessarily implicated in the world (this arises from man's physical condition and the fact that there is interaction between this condition and man's environment), but we also have man's consciousness as something which can be active in a state of free-play. A characteristic and dominant mode of these activities of consciousness is creative activity.

It is my belief that our interest and concern with reality is tied to the demands it makes upon us. In other words our material involvement is something materially necessitated. However, the material necessity we are subjected to is something which in our creative role we are increasingly releasing ourselves from. To believe this is to share in Marxist optimism and to reject contemporary prophecies of doom (i.e. a doom resulting from our technological expertise). The Marxist optimism one is called upon to share is only an optimism which allows man's release from material necessity as a possibility. The more we release ourselves from material necessity, the greater the distance between ourselves and reality, and the greater this distance the more consciousness becomes a world unto itself. Although it has the ring of a paradox, reality holds no intrinsic interest for us. We are interested in it only in so far as it forces us to come to terms with it. Of course, there are particular joys of the senses which on the face of it we do not seem to be forced to seek out, but when we consider the phenomenon as a whole, the seeking of sensations for their own sake does seem something forced on us by our physical make-up and by the way in which it is related to our material environment (e.g. sexual sensations).[60]

But still we are not at the root of the question, for why is it that reality holds no interest for us except where it confines us? The answer to this makes the discussion partly circular. In confronting reality our state becomes precarious and, more-over, we confront something that resists us; this latter factor helps to explain the former. Our natural response in this situation is to extricate ourselves. One way of doing this is to make the reality flexible or pliable, in which case we are in a position to dismiss it. For instance, we may turn it into some functional artefact (e.g. gasometer) and this allows us to ignore it for as long as it continues to satisfy its function. On the other hand, in making it flexible we may turn it into some 'as if' entity and so, though we attend to it, we no longer attend to it as reality. This second way of extricating ourselves depends upon our having the choice of confrontation, and if we have we can retire to a safer, reality-insulated position. It is interesting to reflect that the great palaces and castles of previous societies have tended to fulfil this function. Given the argument, it is also convenient to realise that such palaces and castles have constituted great examples of the world of the 'as if'. We come into contact with reality only to put ourselves at a distance from it, or at least unless it overwhelms us this is the case. The successful human being succeeds in distancing himself from reality, the human being who does not do this falls into an animal existence. Reality is offset, or it is untilised as a means, or it crushes. Of course, for a particular human being nothing is ever so black and white as these alternatives suggest, and what we should really say is that societies are constantly shifting between these states. The tendency is for societies to become more and more successful at distancing themselves from reality, although this is not to say they have no experience of reality as a crushing force.

Having distanced ourselves from reality human existence does not dry up on itself. The existence of an animal is unthinkable unless we think of it in some physical communion with its environment, but the same is clearly not true for man. For man the world of consciousness is a world unto itself. Given the conquest of nature, the dominant mode of human existence would become the gratuitous exercise of man's creative capacities. This would be so because this is what man does when not locked in battle with nature. Whether or not any of this should come to pass is incidental to the proposed question and its answer. If we are asking what is the attraction of independent worlds as given to us in 'entertainment objects', of if we are asking the more focused question, namely, what is the attraction of the patterned meaningfulness of independent worlds, then our present reflections lead us to say such things fit or are natural to a distinctive aspect of our human activity. Without pragmatic justification our minds play with possibilities (if only because we could not have our kind of consciousness without doing this) and the independent worlds of 'entertainment objects' are possibilities produced in this way. They fit or suit one way we have of conceiving of things. The question being asked is akin to asking, if there were gods why should creations attract them, and the answer to this question is that a god's form of existence is to create; it is this, the act of creation and the creation itself, in which he would interest himself.

'Entertainment objects' are important, therefore, because they are fairly complete versions of the kind of objects that our consciousness (possibly the only form of consciousness we can begin to make intelligible to ourselves) constantly aims at. The more reality is distanced the more we fulfil our predisposition. We may reflect that 'entertainment objects' could be conceived of as a primitive form of a life that we might expand upon given a greater distancing of ourselves from reality. Certainly, the unprecedented rise in popular culture has gone hand in hand with the working-classes' comparitive release from material activity. The form of life, which we have now in primitive form, is something speculated about in the final chapter of this book.

12

The 'as if', the real and the defence of art reconsidered

In this chapter I shall consider objections to my argument. The objections that I shall consider all try to root the 'entertainment object' in reality, so that an interest in it is an interest in the reality in which it is alleged to be rooted. Some of these objections would, by these means, try to preserve a distinction between art and the other things included in the category of 'entertainment objects'. An important part of my thesis has been that the 'entertainment object' is something taken on for itself, and not something taken on as a lens through which reality is perceived.

The first objection is very much a philosophical one. It might be argued that the 'entertaiment object' results from thinking, making up, inventing, etc., and what is experienced in engaging in these activities eventually finds its way into the work. The objection might then proceed, therefore the work is about real experience. It may not be about historical events in the world but it is about historical events in the mind. The objection is that necessarily the work *is about real experience* and not just out to make it *seem that it is some real experience*.

The objection, as I have stated it, conceals some ambiguity as to what it is which finds its way into the work. This problem concerns some equivocation over the word 'experience'. If the creation of the object can be said to be an experience its maker has, then it is not this which necessarily finds its way into the work. That this is so entails that the experience of imaginary awareness, which may enter the making process, does not automatically go into the finished object. The real experiences, which the objection holds the work is about, are what the experiences of creation are experiences of. Often we refer to what is experienced as an experience itself (e.g. 'a skylark in flight is a magnificent experience', 'Cairo is the experience of a lifetime') and it is this which is said to find its way, necessarily, into the 'entertainment object'. When we have the objection in this form it fails readily, for what goes

156

into the work is no more and no less than part of the work itself. The work is made up of its parts, and its parts are produced by the maker, but this does not mean that the entrance of these parts into the work has anything to do with the work presenting the historical events in its maker's mind. What is thought up in making the work is not at all the same as descriptions of the making of itself.

This objection leads to another which is less philosophical, but more common. The second objection is the assertion of the 'intentional fallacy fallacy'. If the work is not to be understood as presenting the historical events in the mind of its maker, the objection is that it is to be understood as the maker speaking to the recipient. The claim is: our interest in the 'entertainment object' is an interest in its maker. The view is very much the view of Romanticism, but it is the view of most opponents of Wimsatt and Bearsley's assertion of the intentional fallacy.[61] The Romantic's position can be dismissed fairly easily for when stretched as far as its internal logic compels it is not a thesis about 'entertainment objects', nor even a thesis about art. The Romantic's thesis is a moral thesis about what really matters, and 'entertainment objects' along with everything else, will be judged according to moral priorities. The idea is that a man must be natural in everything he does, and the value of everything he does depends upon it being a true expression of his uncontaminated self. Clearly, 'entertainment objects' can be used as evidence to reveal something of their makers, and there may be circumstances in which we think it more important to inspect them as this kind of evidence than to take them on in any other way. However, this says nothing about what may be involved in taking the object on for itself, or whether or not the object can be so taken on. In this moral position there is no notion of what is the appropriate response to the kind of thing to which the particular object belongs. This objection, therefore, is not to the point.

Opponents of the intentional fallacy thesis argue, sometimes only implicitly, that the object is nothing over and above what its maker is saying. The point is not that morally one ought to take it on in this way, but rather that there is no other way to take it. This thesis has been argued mostly with regard

to literature, and to give it maximum opportunity I will deal
with it on its own ground. It is Cioffi's argument in his article
'Intention and Interpretation in Criticism'[62] that 'The notion
of the author's intention is logically tied to the interpretation
we give to his work.' Thus, when we find ourselves favouring
an interpretation, despite renunciations of it by the author, we
are not supposing the work has a meaning independent of
what the author intends, rather we suppose the interpretation
we favour is what the author intends, whereas his own statement as to its meaning is an aberration: this is Cioffi's position. For him there is an implicit biographical reference in our
response to literature. He allows there are cases where we
might insist on an interpretation yet know the author could
not possibly have intended it, for instance, the Fabian interpretation of 'satanic mills' in Blake's poem, but he thinks
these cases will be confined to an odd word or phrase here and
there. This concession loosens the 'logical tie' between interpretation and intention, unless it is meant to hold between
overall interpretation and overall intention. For Cioffi, at this
level of generality, the tie certainly holds. Thus, it was not a
psychological impossibility on the part of Frank Harris which
prevented him from reading Housman's poem as an anti-
imperialist gibe when he learnt it was seriously intended as a
statement of patriotism, but rather a logical impossibility.
Why should we accept this view? According to Cioffi, if our
interpretation really does not fit the author's intention then
no matter how good the poem comes out on our interpretation, the fact that it does not fit is conclusive against it. Why
should we throw away a perfectly acceptable poem? It seems
extravagant. Of course, Cioffi's objection is not meant as
fussiness, but the only thing which saves it from this is if, for
instance, Housman's poem has (logically) to be understood as
what Housman means or says. But if this is a necessary truth
how does one show it to be so? Why should interpretations of
A's poem necessarily have to take the form, 'A says or
means'? All that 'A's poem' means is that A wrote it. If we
want to know what A means in *his* poem then we must discard
interpretations which A could not possibly have intended, but
why should wanting to know this necessarily coincide with
responding to the poem *qua* poem? If Donne (to take up

another of Cioffi's examples) really had known nothing of the
new astonomy, why should that conclusively settle us on the
earthquake interpretation of the controversial quatrain in
Valediction Forbidding Mourning? It only does if we think
that all our problems about the poem will be resolved eventually in assertions of the form 'Donne says' or 'Donne
means', but what are the *a priori* considerations which bring
us to the necessity of this? Certainly, proponents of the
'intentional fallacy fallacy' fail to exhibit them. To be fair,
proponents of the intentional fallacy take it as obvious that
the interpretation which the text sanctifies will nevertheless
bear the form 'A (the author) means this'. This is Wimsatt's
and Beardsley's position. Perhaps it is the most obvious line to
take, simply because the history of criticism is based on the
format, but there are many reasons for denying it as a
necessary truth.

The case of drama brings out fairly clearly the lack of
necessity. It is very much a tradition in producing a well-worn
play to find a new way of doing it. Sometimes, in this search,
the director concludes that this is what the playwright was
really getting at, but just as often this is of little consequence to him. The important consideration is that the play
can be made to work within the new interpretation. Given a
play can attract innumerable interpretations, that on the
model 'A means or says' would have to be accounted contradictory, it seems absurd to have to play with the idea as to
which of the various productions will be watched no longer.
Cioffi's thesis leads to such absurdities.

It might be argued that the case changes when we come to
poetry, because poetry is experienced as a private, intimate
communication between two persons. But it is not true that all
poetry needs to be experienced in this way, and even in cases
where this is necessary it is not as though one *must* identify the
one who speaks to one as the man who was the poet (i.e. it is
not necessary to ascribe to him the beliefs one must ascribe to
the dramatic speaker).
involved attending to the poet (i.e. focusing on what *he* has to

Even if it was the case that understanding the poem coin-
cided (i.e. had to coincide) with how it was intended, this
would not of itself guarantee that understanding the poem

say or seeing him as communicating with one), for it might be his intention that we treat his poem as something apart from himself and not as a personal statement made to us. And, even in the case where the poem is intended as a personal statement, it is not as though responding to this could characterise responding to poetry, for poetry is something over and above the passionate entreaty we might find in a letter written to ourselves. A poem will be deeply rooted in the 'as if', and this in itself means that the object of our attention cannot be the urgent reality with which the poem may be causally connected. The very fact that a piece of writing is in rhyme and metre works against it as an urgent summons, and puts us into the frame of mind to expect something else from it.

At this point the objections to my argument might become more of a sequence and more summatory. It might be agreed that one can create without the elements of one's creation being locatable in one's previous experience, it may be agreed, also, that one can achieve a likeness to something without there *being* that something and without there *being* something of that kind. Thus, it may be allowed that I am right about how 'entertainment objects' can come into existence, and about how they may be responded to, but, it might be insisted, *there are* works built from reality, reality-directed works, about which the whole point is that we interpret them as reality oriented. The objection might continue that there is a notion of truth which is applied to works of this kind as the standard by which they are judged. This says something about the proper motivation for approaching them, for we should approach them with regard to their cognitive content. There are, at this point, various theories about the kind of cognitive content these works may possess. They may present us with the universal, or they may try to communicate about sensuous experience, or intensely personal and subjective experience. The attempt of these theories is to find some cognitive concern which these works are uniquely about. From here on the objection is not difficult to anticipate. Standardly, the argument proceeds: the importance or significance of these works lies in their conveying the kind of truths which they do; they constitute one other aspect of man's search for knowledge; the class of works concerning themselves with this goal are known as works of art. Thus, the defence of art re-emerges. The argument is that we take on these works as vehicles of knowledge. If we can accept them in this role we account them a success, otherwise we judge them to be failures. If we come across a work that is not to be treated in this way, then we may think of it as entertainment but not as art. Art concerns itself with more serious or profound things, or, if not that, its concern is serious or profound. This argument, therefore, couples truth and art, the former being a necessary condition of the latter, and the latter having as its most serious objective the former. With the argument in this form it is clear how common it is; it is also clear that doctrines of realism are only one form in which the argument is put. Theories about beauty and truth are assertions of the same argument. Consideration of this argument has two strands to it. It must be shown what is wrong with it, but it must also be shown why so many are drawn to it. Both these aims are assisted by taking up a point made earlier in the discussion on convincingness. There, it was suggested the sense of reality conveyed by successful 'entertainment objects' led one to allege correspondence. For instance, if it is asserted of Kipling's *Kim* that it gives a wonderfully penetrating, honest and accurate picture of India at that time, and if this assertion comes, say, from the academic critic who has no experience of Kipling's India, then one is left curious as to the grounds for this assertion. Often, I think, the feeling of reality that the work gives prompts the expectation that correlations exist between the world of the novel and the historical and political circumstances of the same period. Thus, the convincingness of a work can lead to its being thought true.

The ulitmate unimportance of truth, as a condition for judgment, is brought out when we reflect that a work cannot carry its own certificate of truth, for its truth depends upon its fitting the facts, and to determine this we must turn to the facts as well as to the work. In checking up we could go wrong. For those for whom Kipling's novel works, it seems hard to imagine they would give up their view of the work if there were revelations that fundamentally upset long-settled beliefs about the India Kipling knew. Or, to take a more startling case, suppose the First World War was a myth, fed to us by rulers in much the same way as the Platonic myth was intended to be disseminated, what would we then say of the poems of Wilfred Owen? Or, to take a similar though possibly less startling case, suppose Owen had had no direct experience of war, or even more perversely had sadistically enjoyed the entire spectacle? Can these cases really be discounted on the evidence of the poems alone?

To sustain itself the objection gets generalised. It is at this point that special theories about the cognitive content of some 'entertainment objects' (i.e. those which are works of art) is developed. It is argued that the importance of the truths revealed is not that they are specific truths, but that they are truths about areas of human concern conceived of in the most general terms. Thus, it is not that the truths are truths about a specific war, or even that they are about war in general, but rather that they are about human suffering, or human conflict. It is this which makes the poems of Wilfred Owen so fine, or such is the argument. If one asks of the argument in this form for the truths which works of this kind communicate, either they are not forthcoming, or, what one is given is so general and trite as to fail utterly in explaining the work's importance.

However, this is not the end of the argument, for another shift is possible which transforms it into something much more powerful. The shift concerns dropping the idea of the work as a cognitive object and stressing its expressive role. What the argument stresses is the attraction of the authenticity of the expression. An analogy helps to make the argument clearer. We might argue that the hippy and Underground fringes in Western society were more adequate expressions of the total reality of this society than are over-functionally minded members of the bourgeoisie. This point need not be confused with the idea that the Underground's view of society was more sensible than the bourgeois, for we might maintain both viewpoints were in many ways idiotic, and yet maintain the hippy was a better image of the society, or more expressive of its character. Similarly, an old drunk, or a down-and-out, can in himself, be expressive of his time and place more so than say, more average members of the society. If we held this view about hippies we might, as a consequence, feel more drawn to them, or more in sympathy with them, not because they revealed society to us, for we may have more adequate routes to these insights, but because they were more authentic or more faithful to the real situation. It is easy to see how this argument could be adapted so as to distinguish various 'entertainment objects'.

Commendation, according to this theory, is a species of moral admiration. Not in the sense that we think the hippy ethical or morally ideal, but in the sense that he was an adequate expression of the moral character of his society. However, as in other objections, there is here the possibility of musunderstanding the nature of our interest. It seems more likely that one's appreciation would outlast the discovery that the thing in question failed to be an adequate expression of its time in the case of an 'entertainment object', than in the case of a person (e.g. the hippy). If we come to the opinion that the hippy cult was merely a superficial fashion within society then our previous admiration must dissipate, but the same is not so likely to be the case if we consider how we responded to *Look Back in Anger* in the 1950s, and how we respond to it now. In the 1950s it was easier to feel this play was a summation of a whole way of life, that it was an expression equal to the reality and an expression which the reality deserved, whereas it would be more difficult to maintain this now, though the play still seems to work.

However, what of the opponent who is obdurate: He will not have his interest redefined. If he should discover he is mistaken in his assessment of the overall expressiveness of the work, his interest would not survive this. Is this attitude possible? I think it is, for, if there are no clearer cases, certainly many Marxists must commit themselves to this position.

An 'entertainment object' *can* be contemplated as a revealing and authentic object, just as it can be contemplated as a moral object, or again as an economic object. However, a description of this interest is not a description of aesthetic interest *as it exists*; at best it describes a small part of this varied interest. This, then, is not a way of reinstating the category of art as a justifiably superior sub-class of 'entertainment objects'. The experience of art often has little to do

with the appropriateness of the expression to its time and
place.

Yet the moral argument may stand. It may be asserted that
the category of art, *as it exists*, is not a collection of objects
that are adequate expressions of reality and therefore admirable, but that, despite this, there is such a category of objects
and these are the objects of true art. The point of this
argument is prescriptive. The argument is that within the class
of 'entertainment objects' there is a group of superior objects,
objects worthy of our attention, and that these, and only
these, should command our interest, where this interest implies moral approbation. Some Marxists hold this view. The
excluded 'entertainment objects' may be of interest, in so far
as they are symptomatic of class divisions within society, but
they are not to be admired for themselves. If any emotional
attitude is due to them it should be one of pity or scorn.

Why should one be so against works which do not inspire
moral approbation? It is not difficult to see why one might
find oneself against the bourgeois while admiring the hippy;
one might feel it morally negligent to lead so false a life when
conditions in society are as they are, especially when the life
led is very much responsible for the conditions. However,
similar antagonism to works that fail to stimulate the requisite
moral approbation seems quite out of place, for though a
whole life led without genuine regard for the problems of
society may seem morally reprehensible, a whole work that
has other preoccupations seems quite unobjectionable, and
so seems the preoccupation it stimulates. Of course, the
argument may change if we look at the rejected works *en
masse*, and similarly at the mass preoccupation with them, but
if the argument changes it becomes an extremely tenuous one.
The changed argument would talk of the dulling and escapist
character of the mass of popular culture, and indict it for the
social attitudes it inspires, but this is a line of thought which,
though a journalistic cliché, is quite without evidence. It is
not possible to prove connections between violence in 'entertainment objects' and violence in society, let alone prove
something as complex as what this argument requires. Moreover, if this is impossible to prove, how insuperable would be
the problem of showing that escapist works produce these

social consequences intrinsically, and that there could be no society in which such works could be enjoyed independently of their producing such effects?

That works may be morally admired for some reason is not what is disputed. What has been objected to is that in this way it is attempted to reinstate the category of art as rationally determinable. 'Entertainment objects' are necessarily attended to as independent worlds, even though some of them may excite in us moral applause through a perception of their links with reality, but nothing follows from this over and above the fact that such works inspire moral applause.

13

Speculations concerning the 'as if' as a total form of life

At the beginning and end of Antonioni's film *Blow Up* a tribe of seemingly theatrical people (or are they merely students doing Rag?) invade certain non-theatrical, ordinary environments. The situation is a little like the cast of *Hair* taking to the streets. At the end of *Blow Up* these people play out an imaginary game of tennis, imaginary because it is played without racquets or ball. One of the players knocks an imaginary ball over the netting surrounding the court and the film's hero (the trendy photographer), in a moment of reflection on the existence of the artist, picks it up and throws it back. The conclusion he is led to is that he spends his life not in encountering the real but in encountering the 'as if', and making it as real as he can. But more than this, we are given a picture of a form of life we might come to live. The theatical troupe's activities span the duration of the film and because of this it is possible to conclude that this is how they live, that this for them is normality. Their invitation to the photographer is for him to join this form of life, which in a more limited way he has done already, although until that moment without quite knowing it.

To see these scenes in Antonioni's film in this way is to use them as an under-articulated image of the totality of a possible existence. What it is interesting to speculate would be some of the details and possibilities within such an existence? Relating this question to the language of this book we might ask for a description of life if lived wholly within the sphere of the 'as if', where this sphere was communally shared. Of course, we have to hand examples, or cases of separate individuals giving their lives over to an 'as if' world; some such people are artists, who are totally obsessed by their activity, and madmen. Moreover, we have had to hand experimental attempts at setting up communal 'as if' worlds, as was evidenced in the Underground movement. Although these experiments are not consciously directed to the 'as if' in many cases this is what

166

they add up to. What is significant about these experimental activities is not whether they may give rise to enduring results, but that it is in these times that younger people have been moving into such life experiments with frequency and universality.

The existing, though evolving, set of 'entertainment forms' may be seen as the areas in which fragmentary participation in an 'as if' world takes place. The scenes from *Blow Up* my be seen as images of total participation in an 'as if' world that untilises, or requires, an extended use of our present 'entertainment forms'. We may envisage the separateness of the forms giving way to an amalgam of them all, until the possibilities of life become the possibilities of mixed media. Thus, our life with 'entertainment objects' becomes, on this sort of projection, the primitive beginnings of a more complete form of existence, just as the primitive concern with religion can be seen as the beginnings of scientific thought. This would not be to suggest that we are only at the beginning of this process, for the mass preoccupation with popular culture suggests we are far along the road. To detail the intricacies of this line of development from primitive experience until now is a task for another context, what can be detailed now, to a limited extent, is the world imaged in *Blow Up*.

The most remarkable feature of this projection is likely to concern our sense of personal identity. Of course, a person would remain the same person until his death and even then we would have ways of referring to and thinking of that person, but from a point of a personal concern this sense of actual, distinct persons, and their continuity, would fade. Such a conception is removed from social reality as we experience it, though not far removed. For emotional and practical reasons the identification of others, and the presentation of ourselves as practically indentifiable, is necessary to our form of social existence, just as it has been necessary to all forms of social reality until the present time. However, what the images from *Blow Up* induce us to think about is the possibility of the identification of real persons becoming redundant, whilst persons necessarily continue to have an identity. Thus, though identity implies the possibility of identification, it fails to imply the need to identify. Contemporary

society itself makes re-identification of others in many circumstances increasingly irrelevant. Thus, of many persons
whom we pass and with whom we have minor transactions we
develop no identificatory conception. The complex movement of masses of people encourages us in this lack of concern
with others as continuing persons, or, as some might have it,
with others as persons. In our social circumstances the range
of intimate acquaintances is decreasing and in its place has
come a far-reaching alienation of man from man. The normal
view of this alienation has seen it as a social malaise, to be
overcome by means of psychological medicine, of love (Chris-
tian/hippy idea), or revolution. However, we might take
another view of the matter and see it as a progressive feature
in man.

We know, as it might seem seventeenth- and eighteenth-
century political theorists did not, that man's origins were
communal and social. It is not grotesquely far-fetched to see
human development as a very gradual breaking down of
communal relationships and a very gradual emergence of a
desocialised, self-sufficient man. In our present state we
respond to society as a machine, thus, in our social roles,
personal identification becomes increasingly less necessary.
The bus driver needs only to be a bus driver for one to take his
bus, the estate agent needs only to be an obliging voice at the
other end of the telephone for one to buy a house from his
books, etc. A mass of people serve one's needs, but of that
mass only a few are identifiable from one occasion to another.
Clearly, previous forms of society have not been like this,
except at times of particular stress. In our society this dis-
interest in identification has no positive or creative side, it is
simply a consequence of our practical relationships. Thus, it is
not something we make use of to further our private and
collective 'dreams'. *Blow Up* images a different situation. We
might interpret Marx's remarks in *German Ideology* as being
in accordance with this image:

For as soon as labour is distributed each man has a particular,
exclusive sphere of activity, which is forced upon him and from
which he cannot escape. He is a hunter, a fisherman, a shepherd, or
a critical critic, and must remain so if he does not want to lose his

means of livelihood, while in a communist society where nobody has one exclusive sphere of activity but each can become accomplished in any branch he wishes, society regulates the general production and thus makes it possible for me to do one thing today and another tomorrow, to hunt in the morning, fish in the afternoon, rear cattle in the evening, cricize after dinner, just as I have a mind, without ever becoming fisherman, shepherd or critic.[63]

The life imaged becomes a series of roles, where role-playing has reverted to its theatrical context or origins. Therefore, there is a concern with identity, but it is identity in a theatrical guise. Given this became our preconception, then interest in others would be in what they appear to be, rather than in what they are, and this would be of primary concern in self-interest. Man's limits would not be his theatrical limits, his limits would be the limits of the 'as if '. So life would become continuous creative activity. Reality's demands would be left behind as man would transcend his state as victim and become, through himself, his only source of drama; only the dramatic would no longer be a fictionalised gloss concealing the material interaction of man and nature, but instead, a transparent fiction engaged in for its own sake. Man would revert to the play of childhood and engage in it gratuitously. This is a feature of play that psychology is in danger of overlooking in overworking comparisons between the play of animals and the play of children. Here is the possibility of a novel interpretation of Wordsworth's belief that heaven lies about us in our infancy, for heaven, as God's territory, becomes man's play activity as he assumes his god-like role. Thus, *Blow Up*'s image suggests a world in which man's confrontation with reality is at an end, and that, as a consequence, the community of men becomes a community of gods; man moves from 'the kingdom of necessity' to 'the kindom of freedom'. The form of existence envisaged is

one in which music, dance, the making of images, play, pretence, evocation, the construction of narrative, the assumption of theatrical indentities, etc., all synthesise into a continuous free-flowing amalgam constituting the sphere of man. In these circumstances man regains, or becomes his *species being* from which for Marx he has been alienated, and he regains it in what for Marx is its spiritual manifestation (i.e. not merely as a means of life).[64] This is not escapism because there is no pressing reality to escape from, it is merely the natural form of the working of human consciousness in an admittedly far-fetched set of contingencies. What contingencies these are *Blow Up* does not help us with, but what, in general form, I am imagining, and that to which I alluded in an earlier chapter, is the conquest of nature. The ultimate formula for the conquest of nature is a material world controlled by human volition. This is a formula for magic as well, but when the control is mediated by means of causal mechanisms, magic is replaced by science. Although it is not my interest here to make these possibilities plausible (it is enough to sketch the possibilities), it might be mentioned that it is unnecessary to realise a totally flexible universe (i.e. a universe totally amenable to human volition) before the possibilities I am describing become definitive of social existence. The plausibility of these possibilities is brought out by the situation which is, more or less, like a totally flexible universe, for the more the human situation approximates to total control of the material environment, the more plausible it is that life embraces these possibilities. In fact, when we consider man historically we see man, *en masse* today, is much nearer to these possibilities than was man at any other stage, though we must also remark that man remains far removed from a social life that is lived in accordance with these possibilities. Of course, man has engaged in a rich fantasy life in the past, but he has not done so knowingly, and consciousness transforms the nature of the activity. Man's initial fantasies enabled him to accommodate reality, whereas man's ultimate fantasies might spread out around an accommodated reality.

But what would life feel like in this strange world? Can the texture and substance of the life be envisaged and conveyed? We may say the individual cut free from his obsessions with identity (either his own or that of others) would be rootless. He would be an 'easy-rider'. Each man would live out his own Odyssey. The whole of conquered nature would be his hunting ground, and in this world he would move from theatrical adventure to theatrical adventure. Wherever he took himself a person would be and feel secure, therefore, he would have no sense of dependence; instead there would be an overwhelming sense of independence. There would be no need for home or secure relationships, except in so far as one might seek theatrical conceptions of home and intimacy (the Sioux tribe to which one returns, the girl-child one meets in the mountains). As Strawson has pointed out,[65] all-embracing pictures of desirable forms of life are attractive, so much so that alternative and contradictory conceptions often attract the same mind and may secure, only to lose again, the loyalty of that mind. This may go on from month to month, or from week ot week, or from day to day, or even from hour to hour. If we were to probe the phenomenon, I suspect this schizoid tendency would be seen as stemming from the discrepancy between conception and actualisation. The thought of a total life bound by various moral restrictions appeals to our sense of fiction (i.e. the fictions we would weave around our lives), whereas the business of committing the totality of one's life to one plan is experienced as limiting and as challenging one's freedom. Within the projected world the attractions of various forms of life can be responded to without restraints on personal freedom. Vicarious experiences prompted by our own forms of theatrical experience testify to the reality of this possibility.

With the breakdown of our security arrangements (home, intimacy) would come the collapse of a subjective sense of group or social identity. The social universe would be an anarchic collection of seeming individuals and seeming groups, through which one would pass, or with whom one would join in a theatrical sense. Gone, therefore, would be the entities and sets of relationships which keep us stable and restrained. We do not scream, or dance, or sleep, in the streets, and the reason for this is not that we are never so inclined. The reason is much more a matter of the purposes we think society demands of us, or expects us to be about, and the way in which these views count with us. Only individuals who have been forced to the edge of society usually through catastrophe can scream, dance or sleep in the streets (tramps, neurotics, skinheads). The rest of us cannot and cannot because at some point there is a concession to social identity.

The bourgeois intellectual, for instance, tries to lead a life of public dignity, restraint and sophistication, even if laced with private squalor. He will not howl like a dog in front of a Poussin, even if he longs for a more classical order. In public, his behaviour will be controlled, rational and all done with a sort of distant superiority. The novelist's eye is required to convey the tone and no doubt Proust and James give the requisite portraits. For its healthy expression (reduced to a social equal in eccentric circumstances, with, for instance, proletarian non-intellectuals, the bourgeois intellectual becomes withdrawn, inadequate and ill, e.g. T. E. Lawrence as Ross) the life of the bourgeois intellectual requires a coterie of similar minds, all affected with a feeling of superior discernment and taste, even if it is allowed others lack it because they have not had the opportunity to acquire it. Although we could imagine the survival of this life-form in some theatrical reality, its actual existence must prove impossible in the envisaged situation. The structural supports for the belief in the ultimate seriousness of lives like Santayana's are social, and with their removal we see through to the fiction. Where society does not conspire to induce belief in the bourgeois masquerade, then it is experienced as mere masquerade and this, in the projection, is the order of the day. Only where society acts so as to reinforce Santayana's privileges (wealth, solitude) could he become trapped in discernment and dignity. The new situation would liberate us from such traps, for any alternative would be possible and would stand a decision away.

Unfavourably, it might seem these possibilities could be described as an unending, world-wide, pop festival, or as some similar extension of a fancy-dress party, and it would seem the emotional and atmospheric possibilities *would* be similar. In fact, is there anything objectionable in the idea of life being one long party, or one gigantic game, if serious problems have been overcome? There would seem to be a danger of acute inconsistency if we demanded a world which presented serious disturbance. However, at this point there is a movement from a bare description of the possibilities, plus hints about their plausibility, to arguments as to their desirability or otherwise.

Obviously, there are many arguments which might be made

against the desirability of these possibilities. We might point to those activities involving danger and deprivation (a bleak face to face relationship with reality/nature) which men seek out, or we might try some form of religious opposition, or we might argue for the virtues of a life that aimed at being a comprehensive and integrated whole, rather than an arbitrary collection of fragments. However, the only argument I shall consider here is a different one, and concerns what is called 'the search for truth', of which the enterprise of writing this book might be seen to form part.

In the projected life the 'search for truth' seems to have no natural place. For Socrates, so we are asked to believe, the acquisition of knowledge was the highest thing in life and the production of illusion something to be exposed and denounced. In fact, the main tendency in Western 'cultural' culture has been to prefer the Gates of Horn to those of Ivory. The general argument for this preference has turned on the deceptive qualities of the Gates of Ivory compared with the illumination of the Gates of Horn. However, this argument fails to bear on the desirability of the projection, for, in the projected world, illusion (if for a moment we call it that) is enjoyed as illusion, thus, it has no tendnecy to become delusive. Of course, this is not the end of the matter, for a life knowingly devoted to illusion is not a life devoted to knowledge (the understanding of reality), and it is this which our 'cultural' culture has seen as the highest good or the most worthy pursuit, or at least this is how it formulates its values.

It is surprising how widespread is this simple assertion of an ideal, in fact, it is very much an axiom of the cultural liberal, yet such an axiom needs extensive modification, if only because our projects must grow out of the specific features of our time and place and, thus, must be defined in terms of them. In other words, specific environments have created specific needs which have led to specific results (e.g. a philosophical system, a scientific theory), and the net outcome of these various fragments has given man a better understanding of reality than was possessed by his predecessors. There has never been some solid, transcendental realm of truth which we have been systematically and consciously revealing, rather, men have dealt with their own specific concrete problems and their performances have made little sense apart from these problems.

To understand what the so-called seekers of knowledge have done, we must enquire not only into how near the truth they were, or how much nearer the truth they were than their contemporaries, but also into what factors inclined them to behave as they did. It is surely too easy, but more importantly incorrect, to see Socrates and Descartes as compelled into their activities by similar motives. Certainly, both declared they sought truth but what really needs uncovering is what, in their respective social contexts, made their careers possible options for them both. It is unlikely we should find similar stories, for the details we want are ingrained in such different social realities. In the case of Descartes, for instance, we should have to relate his needs for solitude, and his disposition toward meditative activity, to the various alternatives and possibilities within the specific social environment in which he lived. For instance, we would need to ponder very deeply the full, personal and social implications of his delight in his perceptions of reified business men in Amsterdam.

In this great city, where everyone except me is engaged in business, each is so worried about his own profit that I could remain here my entire life without ever being seen. I go for walks every day in the confusion of the great crowds with as much freedom and repose as you would find in your parks and I consider the men whom I see just like trees or animals in your forests.[66]

Descartes 'search for truth' will be mediated by all sorts of things that inclined him towards the life surrounding the 'search for truth', or rather his 'search for truth' would have been this life. In the case of Socrates the chances of piecing his story together are remote, but from what details we possess it seems fairly clear we should have to narrate something very different. This is not just the claim that Socrates life was not that of Descartes. What is being said is that what philosophy meant to them, and why it constituted a possible life for them, was so very different. Philosophising for Descartes meant becoming part of the philosophical practices of his time, similarly for Socrates, but here we find divergent ways of life.

Thus, in Descartes's case we should have to investigate the way the life connected with the institutions of religion, and the way it influenced the practice of philosophy. This enquiry would involve discovering what philosophy was in the seventeenth century. In a similar way it would be necessary to detail the philosophical traditions inherited, i.e. we would have to see what factors in the contemporary scene made certain philosphical traditions viable and others not. All of this would be in addition to the usual story we tell about one who 'seeks truth', namely, the description of the particular intellectual vistas encountered along the route. However, these various perspectives would form an integral whole, a totality, and not merely an addition of items; each perspective would be modified by all of the others. The situation would be no different if the case taken was that of a mathemetician, or chemist, or astronomer, etc.

The 'search for truth' is not an independent activity springing from some unambiguous, ubiquitous motive, but an activity explained by the contingencies on which it depends. This being so, it is logically open that the search could come to an end, or be found irrelevant. Such a state of affairs might well coincide with the conquest of nature, and consequent feelings of self-sufficiency and independence. But is it possible, for instance, that all those engaged in laboratory experiments could ever collectively withdraw from their investigations? Why not? Collective analysis is a very recent phenomenon, and what calls individuals to it is not the 'search for truth' but the way of life which it is, and this way of life has everything to do with the economic forms which make it possible and which act as its rationale.

But is it possible we should ever set aside problems concerning, for instance, the nature of man, or the relationships between experience and reality? Are not such interests in reality fundamental to the human condition? These questions ask whether or not philosophical problems (which are posed as problems about reality) are not in some way fundamental in human consciousness. However, particular philosophical problems would be odd problems if they were genuinely perennial and inherently insoluble, which is to say under such circumstances their relationship to the 'search for truth' would be suspect. Moreover, we would need a special argument, and one we do not have, if it was to be maintained that human reality will always generate philosophical interest in it: assertions about the metaphysical origins of science will be insufficient to establish this argument because they presuppose continuing scientific enquiry. Of course, each man coming into the world blank would not know what philosophy teaches, but then, as I have tried to indicate, philosophy is not simply what it teaches; it is not just a string of truths or a complex of arguments. It is a whole system of conduct, and whether or not an individual would stand in need of such a life would depend on all sorts of things outside some neutral search for truth. If there should be a body of philosophical truths that are needed for a general accomodation of reality, then practices guaranteeing their acquisition would not presuppose some evolutionary activity which we might refer to as 'the search for truth'.

The point in dealing with this objection has been to suggest that we should not too readily assume the necessity of the serious life, or the serious world. The prospect of social life becoming an highly developed form of play is not clearly threatened by the fact of serious intellectual endeavour, and yet this fact might well constitute its ultimate challenge. If, instead of arguing against assertions of undesirability, we were to *indicate* the full and absorbing quality of the life sketched in these projections, then we should have to explain the forms of the 'as if' which we know, and our preoccupation with them. This I have tried to do.

14

Concluding remarks

The fact that we have the ability to conceive of the 'as if' is a central feature of human consciousness. Imagining, and being able to think of what is not the case, are clear instances of how fundamental this ability is to human thought. We can make it as though things are impinging upon consciousness when they are not, and this ability is one we put to use in a variety of ways. One of the possibilities for us, in this respect, is the creation of 'as if' worlds that there is the possibility of us entering for their own sake. We can create situations and objects that are not the same as other situations and objects but which are like them. Moreover, we can see and respond to the likenesses we create although knowing that they are only likenesses. This situation is that where (to put the point in the form of a formula) 'x only seems to be y', and where we are interested in x because it only seems to be y. In the Greek world there was a clearer recognition of the nature of this interest of ours than is present in our world. Both Plato and Aristotle tried to understand the art of imitating. This art is one we have lost sight of in our insistence on focusing on *Art*. For this reason we misinterpret Plato and Aristotle in supposing that they tried to understand *Art* through the concept of imitation, when in fact their interest was in the art of imitating.

'Imitating' is, however, too narrow an idea with which to comprehend the 'as if'. It suggests that 'as if' creations are tied to the way reality is, when the truth is that the 'as if' can go beyond the normal or even the abnormal ways of the world. That their accent was on imitation led both Plato and Aristotle to evaluate imitations by the criterion of truth. Whereas it is an important fact about the 'as if' that it can be very convincing despite there being a lack of correspondence between it and reality. The truth of this points to the subtle ways in which the formula 'x only seems to be y' has to be understood.

In the world as it is we encounter 'as if' situations and objects in reading novels and poems, in listening to music, in looking at pictures and sculptures, in watching films, plays and dancing, and in participating in the making of these things. The novel and the poem make it as though we live through a range of experiences when we do not. Music transports us into a world of quasi-feelings and makes the world take on appearances that it does not possess. The picture and the sculpture necessarily look like something other than they are. The play and the film involve us in a pretend-life, and the dance transforms the dancer into a being other than he or she is.

This existing 'as if' world might be confused with the sphere of art or high culture, but it extends beyond this. The novel, the poem, music, the picture, the sculpture, the play, the film and the dance are not exclusively the objects of high culture, they have more mundane settings for the most part. The 'as if' is not then an élitist practice, although it contains élitist areas. Justifications for the élitist area deride an interest in the mere semblance of a reality. Art tends to be seen as being almost accidentally mimetic in form and its real significance is sought in a baffling array of theories. However, the truth about art is that its real meaning has to be understood as an exclusive and intentionally socially differentiating, social process, whereas theories of art offered within art are obfuscating rationalisations. Moreover, derision of the 'as if' as a facile semblance of reality, is a serious underestimate of its meaning.

The 'as if' as we experience it, in all its forms and all its social settings gives rise to convincing feelings of meaningfulness and completeness. It creates the possibility of a turning away from the open-ended, unsatisfactory character of reality, and creates the possibility of entering into a free, penaltyless situation of convincing semblance. Moreover, such ''as if' worlds constitute the natural form of expression for our creative capacities, when these capacities are released from grappling with the situation of material scarcity. These are some of the obvious and existing benefits we derive from the 'as if'.

There is, however, the possibility of the 'as if' being more than this. The forms in which it appears in existing circumstances can be regarded as primitive embryos. There is the possibility of stitching together all the techniques we have developed for producing the 'as if' so as to yield a total life devoted to the 'as if'. This would be a world of continuous theatre, music and dance in which all our existing preoccupations would give way to a life of knowing pretence and artifice. A necessary pre-condition of this possibility would be a world in which we were released from the dominance of reality and material adversity. To speculate about this might seem idle, but then the unending war that has been waged historically against material adversity should add up to more, in a successful culmination, than mere appetitive and sentient satisfaction. Some theory of life, involving our freedom and creativity, and being about that which is beyond the 'kingdom of necessity' is requisite. The world of the 'as if', as something beyond art and the art forms as they exist (i.e. beyond the world of 'entertainment objects') is a world that provides uncharted scope for speculation, and even in its embryonic form the 'as if' is an area about which the human race is, and always has been, clearly passionate.

Notes

1   R.L. Taylor, *Art an Enemy of the People*, Harvester, Hassocks, 1978.
2   Jean Gimpel, *The Cult or Art*, in translation, London, 1969.
3   Raymond Williams, *Marxism and Literature*, Oxford, 1977.
4   R. Williams's *Marxism and Literature* gives a very general account of how this might be done.
5   H. Marcuse, *Eros and Civilisation*, Boston, 1955, London, 1969.
6   T. Kuhn, *The structure of Scientific Revolutions*, Chicago, 1970.
7   P. Feyerabend, *Against Method*, London, 1975.
8   G. Berkeley, *The Principle of Human Knowledge*, Library of Liberal Arts, 1957.
9   These views are not without critics. They are, for example, in part denied by J. Hospers in his *An Introduction to Philosophical Analysis* (see page 83, revised edn).
10   E.g. S.T. Coleridge in *Biographia Literaria*, Oxford, 1907 and P.B. Shelley in *Defence of Poetry*, London, 1948.
11   R.G. Collingwood, *The Principles of Art*, Oxford, 1938.
12   B. Croce, *Aesthetics*, 2nd edn, in translation, London, 1923.
13   M. Macdonald, 'Art and Imagination', *Proceedings of the Aristotelian Society*, 1952-3.
14   Early versions of this are written into classics of empiricism like Locke's *Essay Concerning Human Understanding*, but equally one can find traces of the theory in Descartes' *Meditations*.
15   L. Wittgenstein, *The Blue and Brown Books*, page 4, 3rd edn, Oxford, 1964.
16   The terminology used is very much that of D. Hume's *Treatise on Human Nature*. For a modern but more complex account read B. Russell *Logic and Knowledge*.
17   *S.T. Coleridge, op.cit*.
18   For a more modern formulation of this see J. Hospers, *Meaning and Truth in the Arts*, Chapel Hill, 1946.
19   For example, R. Descartes, *Meditations*.
20   For example, see W. K. Wimsatt Jr and M. Beardsley, 'The Intentional Fallacy' in *The Verbal Icon* by W.K. Wimsatt, Lexington, 1954.
21   For example, E.H. Gombrich, *Art and Illusion*, New York, 1960, London 1962.
22   L.L. Whyte, *The Unconscious Before Freud*, London, 1962.
23   J.P. Sartre, *The Psychology of the Imagination*, translation, London, 1949, New York 1966.
24   Compare G. Ryle, *Concept of Mind*, London, 1949, or J.P. Sartre, *The Imagination: a psychological critique*, translation, Michigan, 1962.

25 H. Vaihinger, *The Philosophy of 'As If '*, New York, 1925.
26 J.L. Austin, 'Pretending' in his *Philosophical Papers*, Oxford, 1961.
27 E. Bedford, 'Emotion' in *Proceedings of the Aristotelian Society*, Suppl. Vol. 32, 1957-8.
28 E. Anscombe, 'Pretending' in *Proceedings of the Aristotelian Society*, Suppl. Vol. 32, 1957-8.
29 Peter Ansorge, *Disrupting the Spectacle:* Five years of experimental and fringe theatre in Britain, London, 1975.
30 T.E. Hulme, *Speculations*, London, 1936.
31 R.H. Fogle, *The Imagery of Keats and Shelley*, Hamden, 1962.
32 I.A. Richards, *The philosophy of Rhetoric*, London, 1936, New York, 1965.
33 Ryle, *Op cit*.
34 Sartre, *op cit*.
35 Apparently this 'clearly' is not so clear to professional historians.
36 Some of what I mean, though also some of what I do not mean, is contained in the Abbess' remarks in Muriel Sparks', *The Abbess of Crewe*, (p. 104)   ' "... Think up your best scenarios, Sisters" "What are scenarios?", says Winifrede "They are an art-form," says the Abbess of Crewe, "based on facts. A good scenario is a garble. A bad one is a bungle. They need not be plausible, only hypnotic, like all good art" '.
37 M. Macdonald, 'The Language of Fiction', in *Proceedings of the Aristotelian Society*, Suppl. Vol. 27, 1954.
38 Gombrich, *op cit*.
39 R. Wollheim, *On Drawing an Object*, Inaugural Lecture, University College London, 1964.
40 This attempt is more clearly displayed in *Art and its Objects*, New York, 1968.
41 Wollheim produces a footnote to this paragraph making it clear that this is a view he attributes to Gombrich.
42 E.H. Gombrich, *Meditations on a Hobbyhorse*, London, 1963.
43 E.H. Gombrich, 'Meditations on a Hobbyhorse' in *ibid*.
44 A Stokes, *Reflections on the Nude*, London, 1967.
45 Wollheim, *Art and its Objects*.
46 Ibid p. 28.
47 Ibid. p. 14.
48 These qualities are taken from Sibley's list of aesthetic concepts in 'Aesthetic Concepts', *The Philosophical Review*, October 1959. His lists contain many other qualities indicating the 'as if ' character of the object of which they were predicated, e.g. sentimental, tragic, lifeless.
49 H.J. Eysenck, *Sense and Nonesense in Psychology*, Harmondsworth, 1957.
50 J. Hospers, 'Art and Reality' in *Art and Philosophy*, ed. S. Hook, New York, 1966.
51 V. Nijinsky, *The Diary of Nijinsky*, London, 1963.
52 See F. Kermode, *The Romantic Image*, chapter on The Dancer, London, 1957.

53   Hospers, 'Art and Reality'.

54   A. Danto, 'Imagination, Reality and Art' in *Art and Philosophy*.

55   M.H. Abrams, 'Belief and the Suspension of Disbelief' in *Literature and Belief*, ed. M.H. Abrams, New York, 1958.

56   C. Brooks, 'Implications of an Organic Theory of Poetry' in *Literature and Belief*.

57   F. Kermode, *The Sense of an Ending*, New York, 1967, London 1968.

58   Hospers, *Meaning and Truth in the Arts*.

59   Compare Kermode, *The Sense of an Ending*.

60   R.L. Taylor, 'Sexual Experiences', *Proceedings of the Aristotelian Society*, 1967.

61   See Wimsatt and Beardsley, 'The Intentional Fallacy'.

62   F. Cioffi, 'Intention and Interpretation in Criticism', *Proceedings of the Aristotelian Society*, Vol. 14, 1963-4.

63   K. Marx and F. Engels, *German Ideology*, p. 22, Pascal edn, New York, 1947.

64   K. Marx, *Economic and Philosophical Manuscripts*, translation, London, 1959, New York, 1964.

65   P,F. Strawson, 'Freedom and Resentment', 1962 British Academy Lecture in *Philosophy of Thought and Action*, ed. P.F. Strawson, Oxford, 1968.

66   R. Descartes, *Correspondence*, Vol. 1, ed. C. Adams and G. Milhead, Paris, 1951-63.

Index